TWICE PARDONED

An Ex-Con Talks
to Parents and Teens

HAROLD MORRIS

with Dianne Barker

Publishing

Pomona, California

To my mother, Lucille Morris Wiggins,
who consistently lives with
courage and dignity.
As she visited me in prison,
I saw sorrow in her eyes but never shame.

To the memory of my friend, Russell Moore,
whose faith, compassion, patience, and love
demonstrated the matchless power of Christ.
His life taught me to trust.
His death taught me to hope.

TWICE PARDONED: An Ex-Con Talks to Parents and Teens

Copyright © 1986 by Focus on the Family

The names and descriptions of many of the people in this book have been changed to protect their identities.

Library of Congress Cataloging-in-Publication Data

Morris, Harold.
  Twice pardoned.

  1. Morris, Harold. 2. Prisoners—United States—Biography.
3. Ex-convicts—United States—Biography. I. Barker, Dianne.
II. Title.
HV6248.M7773A3   1986   365'.6'0924 [B] 86-12051
ISBN 0-929608-01-1

Published by Focus on the Family Publishing, Pomona, California 91799. Distributed by Word Books, Waco, Texas.

Unless otherwise noted, Scripture quotations are taken from The New King James Version, copyright © 1979, 1980, 1982. Thomas Nelson, Inc., Publishers.

Printed in the United States of America.

89 90 91 92 / 12 11

CONTENTS

FOREWORD

Were it not for a tape given to me in 1983 by former Denver Bronco Randy Gradishar, I may have never become acquainted with Harold Morris. That cassette, recorded before a high school assembly in North Carolina, detailed Harold's roaches-to-heavenly-riches testimony. Much like this book, it presented his gripping personal account of how he, as a promising all-star athlete, got involved in life's rat race, made some wrong choices, and wound up in a dank prison cell with a double life sentence. With hands and feet bound and shackled, he was ushered into Georgia State Penitentiary for what became the worst, and the most blessed, years of his life. And it was there, while surrounded by hardened and perverse criminals, that he experienced the life-changing power of Jesus Christ for the first time.

For an hour, I was held absolutely spellbound as this somewhat brash, always candid ex-con related how that divine meeting transformed his life. And for the entire time, I couldn't help but wish more people could hear what he was saying. Especially parents and teens. Though the closest brush most people have with the law is when they spot a flashing red light in their rearview mirror, I knew they would be challenged by this man who eventually found eternal life just a few cellblocks away from death row. So, with that in mind, I broadcast that same cassette tape in February 1984 on the hundreds of radio stations airing our "Focus on the Family" program.

Well, as the saying goes, the rest is history. Focus on the Family's offices in Arcadia, California, were flooded with thousands of letters the following week. Some were written on sheets of school notebook paper; others on flowery stationery or corporate letterhead. Some, scribbled with felt pens, were almost illegible. Some were typed. They were postmarked from all around the world—from sprawling metropolitan areas and trendy resorts, to small towns and, yes, from prisons and jails throughout North America. Yet, no matter where they were written, each letter conveyed a very personal account of the dramatic impact this one man, Harold Morris, had on people's lives as the result of that single broadcast. Indeed, the final letter count proved to be a record for the radio program. Amazingly, we eventually received and *answered* (after weeks of finger-numbing work by correspondence assistants, I might add), more than 15,000 letters in response to this single message.

Since then, I have come to know Harold as a close friend, a Christian brother, and a valued partner in our efforts on behalf of the family. And recently, I had the opportunity to hear him present his dramatic message to a congregation of families and teenagers at my own church. The audience in the 2,500-seat auditorium was rapt with attention as Harold spoke. Afterward, he asked those present if they, like him, had made some wrong choices along the way. Did they know what it was like to lie awake in bed at 3 A.M., staring at the ceiling because of overwhelming guilt and regret in their lives? Or, alternatively, to cry themselves to sleep night after long, lonely night because of some past mistake or sin? The church was quiet as he continued, explaining to the youth that wrong choices, actions, and thoughts were forgivable; that they, too, could be pardoned for their sins and be set free; that they could personally experience, as he had back in his roach-infested cell, the transforming power and love of Jesus Christ. Harold then invited the young people to come to the front of the church for a prayer of repentance and dedication to the Lord. Teenagers everywhere rose from their seats and walked forward to stand in front of Harold . . . and to meet their Savior. It was a very meaningful moment in the ministry of this unique man.

Having talked at great length with Harold about his motives and his work, I have come to understand the driving force in his life. It is nothing more complex than a desire to serve the Lord and help others avoid the snares that led to his utter humiliation as convict #62345. Hopefully, none of us will ever know what it is like to be stripped, shorn of hair, tossed behind bars, and told we will die in that stinking place. But for millions of teenagers and adults, another kind of prison has walled them in . . . a prison of sin. They are enslaved by drugs, alcohol, sex, and the lust for pleasure. Harold wants to point each of them to the same Jesus Christ who removed his chains and set him free. It is a message of hope that is desperately needed by the present generation.

Whether you're a teen or parent, whether you're married or single, whether you live in a college dorm, warm home, or a cold prison cell, the book you're about to read is the story of a man whose advice should be heeded. A seemingly ordinary man who found himself in extraordinary trouble. And I am grateful to call him my friend.

James C. Dobson, Ph.D.
President, Focus on the Family

ACKNOWLEDGMENTS

It is customary for an author to express gratitude to those who have helped with his book. This being an autobiography, I must thank those who have helped with my life. Would space permit, I'd list the names of all the faithful ones who ministered in Jesus' name along the way I've come!

Friends who believed in me when my world had fallen apart, thank you for love, wisdom, and courage.

Friends who stood in the gap during the initial dark days of my illness, thank you for teaching by example.

My Board of Directors, thank you for devotion in promoting the gospel of Jesus Christ.

Bobby Richardson—one who is not ashamed of the gospel of Christ—thank you for being a friend to Jesus and to me.

My brother Carl Morris and your loving wife, Betty, thank you for loyalty and for loving me through it all.

Dr. James Dobson and the special people at Focus on the Family, thank you for your encouragement, words of wisdom, and confidence in me.

Friends who helped pray this book into being, and my co-author, Dianne Barker, please accept my heartfelt thanks.

CHAPTER 1

MURDER ONE

"Drive! Drive! We shot a man!" shouted my friends as they scrambled down the street toward my car.

I gunned the engine and, without waiting for an explanation, spun the car around and headed in the very direction from which Jack and Danny had come.

"You fool! You're going to get us caught!" Danny yelled. The two men slumped in the backseat as several police cars and an ambulance sped into a supermarket parking lot, their lights flashing and their sirens blaring.

I made a right turn on Ponce de Leon Avenue—the only route I knew out of Atlanta—and took the Interstate north. For some time all I could hear was the rapid breathing of my friends in the backseat, and my head pounded with questions.

A shooting! How could this have happened?

When Jack and Danny finally started to relax, they told me the story. They had walked into the supermarket, pulled guns, and ordered the manager to open the safe. As one of them grabbed a handful of money from the cash register, a bystander reached in his belt and produced a snub-nosed .38 pistol. There was a scuffle, and the would-be hero was shot.

Fun is one thing, I thought, *but being involved in a supermarket robbery—suppose that man dies! Should I go to the police?*

"Did you kill him?" I asked, afraid to hear the answer.

"Nah!" Jack answered, sniffing. "He took it in his side, but he was standing when we ran out. He'll live."

I breathed a sigh of relief. At least the wound wasn't fatal, and I was glad that no one had seemed to notice us when we drove by the supermarket. Although I felt remorse for the wounded man, the farther we got from Atlanta, the more reassured I became. He would recover, I reasoned, and we had escaped. Everything would work out all right. I drew support for my feelings from my friends.

Jack and Danny seemed to think the incident was closed, and they didn't take my concern for the man seriously. They wanted to stop for food and beer, and then they slept while I drove the 350 miles to my home in Greensboro, North Carolina. The six-hour drive gave me plenty of time to review the events of the past few months.

I had met Jack and Danny at a topless nightclub in Greensboro shortly after separating from my wife. The idea of spending the rest of my days with one woman had lost its appeal, and I made no secret of my drinking and girl chasing. After the divorce, I began spending a lot of time at the nightclub, the first topless club in the state of North Carolina. It was a fast life, and I was running—but I didn't know where.

I had a respectable job with an insurance company, a new Cadillac, and the freedom I thought I wanted. I had never been in trouble with the police, not even a ticket for parking or speeding, and I'd never seen an ex-convict. But that soon changed. The nightclub attracted the shadiest of characters— hardened alcoholics, drug addicts, drug pushers, ex-cons, and prostitutes. This life was new to me, and I found myself falling deeper and deeper into the mire.

While I put up a good front for my new friends, inside I was miserable and confused. My drinking increased until my days and nights were consumed with alcohol and women. I discovered amphetamines, and pills called "black beauties" soon became a part of my life.

Finally, I quit my job. A little money trickled in from insurance policies that I had sold, but it was not enough to support my lavish lifestyle. I worked a few hours at the nightclub and lived on credit cards, running up debts totaling several thousand dollars.

Shortly thereafter, my girlfriend introduced me to Jack. He and his friend, Danny, were sharp dressers, fast talkers, and big spenders. They were also handsome and popular with women. The three of us hit it off immediately, and Jack invited me to move in with him.

I didn't know that he was an ex-convict. All Jack told me was that he had "connections." That's how he explained having 500 new suits (he assured me the clothes weren't "hot"). Although I wanted to believe him, I was certain they were stolen. Nevertheless, I rationalized away my concerns and bought several. I sold others to friends.

One night, Jack asked me to pick him up at the Holiday Inn at 9:30. For that small favor, he gave me $2,000. The next day I read in the newspaper that the motel had been robbed. When I asked Jack about it, he said, "Don't ask questions. You were well paid." I was scared, but I was also heavily in debt, so I kept the money and remained silent. I should have gone to the police, but sleeping during the day and partying all night gave my conscience little time to work.

Tiring of the Greensboro party scene, my two friends and I sought women and excitement in other cities, from Myrtle Beach to New York. Jack always had pocketfuls of money, and sometimes he picked up the tab for the entire week. The nightlife in Atlanta lured us like moths to a flame, so we went there often.

On September 18, 1968, we checked into a room at the Heart of Atlanta Motel, and then hit one nightclub after another while high on alcohol and pills. After a week of this, we'd spent our cash, leaving only credit cards to cover our expenses. I was ready to return to North Carolina, anyway. So on the 25th we checked out of the motel. Before leaving town, my friends insisted on visiting some girls we had met earlier in the week.

I drove to the address they had given us—North Highland Avenue. We knocked on the door but no one answered. As we waited in the car for the girls to come home from work, Jack and Danny left me unexpectedly and started down the street, saying they would be right back.

Soon the girls arrived, and I went inside the apartment with them. Minutes after I returned to the car, Jack and Danny came racing down the street, breathless and obviously shaken, shouting that they'd just shot a man.

But now we were approaching Greensboro, and neither Jack nor Danny seemed shaken anymore. As they dozed in the backseat, my confidence gave way to doubts. I fell deeper and deeper into despair.

You've reached the bottom of the barrel now, I told myself. *Dad always said you'd never amount to anything. Maybe he was right. But maybe he wasn't right,* I reasoned. *And if that's true, I'll have to break away from Jack and Danny if I'm ever going to do something with my life.*

Weeks earlier, I had moved out of Jack's place to share an apartment with the nightclub owner. That would make it easier to leave them now. I dropped the men off at Jack's apartment, making no mention of my plans to leave town. Then I gathered my things and drove to Houston, Texas, where a friend had offered to share his apartment.

I was there only a few days when my friend suddenly accepted a new job in Atlanta. With no other connections in Houston, I decided to move with him. I heard nothing more about the shooting and put the incident out of my mind.

Although I was removed from my former friends, I did not break from the women-and-booze lifestyle. In Atlanta I hit the party scene heavier than ever. The months passed, and I almost totally forgot the robbery until an old girlfriend called from North Carolina.

"You made the front page today," she said.

"What do you mean?"

"Your picture is on the front page of the newspaper. You're wanted for armed robbery and murder."

"Murder!" I gasped. My stomach tightened as the reality hit home. Jack and Danny *had* killed the man in the supermarket.

"The FBI has been questioning me, Harold," she said. "They say the man you shot only lived five minutes."

"I didn't shoot anybody!" I protested.

"Well, your two friends are locked up, and the police are looking for you."

When our conversation ended, I sat thinking about the night of the robbery. I knew I was guilty of some despicable things, but I wasn't a robber or a murderer. I hadn't run from the authorities, and I wasn't hiding now. I waited in Atlanta for several days, expecting the officers to come for me. When they didn't, I decided to return to North Carolina to see an attorney friend. We had played the party scene together, and I thought I could trust him to find out what was going on.

The attorney had already heard of the charges against me, and he wanted to know about my involvement in the crime. He said he believed my story, but he advised me to wait for a while before going to the police. First he would check around the courthouse to see what the two captured suspects were saying. Then I'd go to the police and tell everything. For testifying against them, I'd probably be freed, he said. After all, I had been implicated simply because I knew them; I hadn't killed anybody. There was no problem, he assured me.

When I called the attorney a few days later, he seemed baffled. Everyone was hush-hush about the case, he said, but he had learned that Jack and Danny were not in the local jail. He needed more time, and it seemed important to find out what was going on before turning myself in to the police. I'd risk arrest if I stayed in Greensboro or if I returned to Atlanta, so my only alternative was to run.

I sold my car for traveling money and rode to Myrtle

Beach with a friend. After several days of partying there, we went to Charleston, Savannah, Columbia, and finally to Greenville, South Carolina, where my friend left me, saying he would return in a few days. On his way back to North Carolina, he was stopped for speeding, and to avoid losing his license he made a bargain. In return for having the traffic charge dropped, he would help solve a murder. He told the officer where to find me. I was staying at a motel with a girl I'd met in Columbia, but we had separate rooms so I would be free to see other women.

On September 18—one year after the shooting in Atlanta—I returned to the motel about 8 A.M. after spending all night with a new girlfriend. When she dropped me off, I bought a Pepsi and a newspaper on the way to my room. Sitting by the window to read, I closed the draperies about ten o'clock, latched the door, and settled into bed. Thirty minutes later a knock awakened me. Groggy with sleep, I opened the door but found no one there. Thinking it must have been the maid, I dozed off again.

Bam! Bam! Bam!

The maid again! I was really agitated over being bothered a second time. As I unfastened the night latch, the door was kicked open, and a dozen officers burst into the room, thrusting pistols against my head.

"If you move, you're dead!" they shouted, throwing me to the bed and handcuffing my hands behind my back.

"Where's the gun?" they demanded, emptying dresser drawers and wastebaskets. I had never owned a gun in my life. The scene taking place before me could have been from a gangster movie—and I was playing a part.

"Take him downtown and book him," snapped the officer in charge.

"Are you going to carry me out naked?" I objected as they grabbed my arms and started to push me out the door.

"Put some clothes on," he said.

"How do you expect me to dress? Do you think I can stretch like Gumby?" I quipped.

They loosened one hand so I could get into my clothes.

"How about my money?" I asked.

"Count his money. The ------ thinks he's smart," someone grumbled.

"Listen, you've got me. All I want is my money and what belongs to me," I said. They never knew about the girl in the next room.

During the drive to the county jail, they bombarded me with questions. "When did you get into town? What have you been doing?" On and on they pressed, insisting I give them the information they wanted. Knowing I had the right to have an attorney present during questioning, I answered nothing.

When we arrived at the jail, the officers became furious when I objected to being fingerprinted. Threatened with a beating, I finally agreed. Arraignment was before a federal magistrate, who set bond at $10,000. There, I learned that I was charged with armed robbery in Greensboro. That really threw me.

How could I be wanted for an Atlanta murder, which I did not commit, but charged with a Greensboro robbery, which I knew nothing about? I figured the officers didn't know about the murder. By raising a $10,000 bond, I could be free.

I used the one phone call that I was allowed to contact an attorney recognized as one of the best in the state of South Carolina. His secretary said it would cost $200 just to talk with him. I had $500 in cash. The attorney, however, was out of town, and it would be several days before he could see me.

About two hours later an FBI agent came to my holding cell and wiped out all hope for an early release.

"Harold Morris, I have something to read to you," he said. He read six indictments for armed robbery and one for murder.

"There is no bond," he announced.

The other men in my cell were relieved. Because I was

stylishly dressed in a double-breasted sports jacket, they had thought I was an informant planted by the FBI. They planned to stab me, one told me later. But when those charges were read, they decided I was a desperado much more dangerous than any of them.

Six armed robberies, murder one, no bond. How could this have happened to me? I had seen myself as a country boy who had made it to the big time. I had adopted a playboy lifestyle because it promised me the freedom to do whatever I pleased. *This must be a hideous nightmare,* I told myself. *When I wake up, everything will be okay.* But the jail bars told me otherwise.

CHAPTER 2

DOUBLE LIFE

For three days I sat in a filthy jail cell, trying to sort out the puzzle of my existence. I had failed in every area of my life—school, work, marriage. Even athletics had proven to be an illusion. And now my choice of friends had plunged me into a nightmare.

I was still wearing the clothes I'd scrambled into when I was taken into custody. On the third day after my arrest, a policeman took me to a room where two FBI agents delivered my toiletries from the motel. A radio and some other personal items were missing, but I didn't mention it to the two men. Instead, I signed a form releasing them of responsibility for my possessions.

"You're not what we expected," one said. "You're a pretty decent guy—not the kind who would do the things you're accused of doing."

"What happens next?" I asked.

"You were arrested for interstate flight to avoid prosecution. You'll be turned over to the authorities in North Carolina first and Georgia later. You're really in trouble. The case is out of our hands, and we won't be back."

"We do have one question," the other agent added. "Looking over your personal things, we found a woman's wig, pantyhose, panties, and shoes. I don't understand. What are you doing with a woman's clothes?"

They still didn't know about the girl at the motel! By that time I had lost everything except my sense of humor.

"Don't you know?" I said, my expression serious. "I'm a drag queen."

"Get him out of here," the first agent snapped to the guard.

I laughed all the way back to my cell, but then I stopped. I had no idea what was in store for me.

My attorney was still away when Greensboro detectives came to interrogate me. They began with a friendly approach, trying to win me over while building a case against me. When I refused to talk with them or to sign extradition papers, their approach changed to cursing and threatening.

Finally, I talked with my attorney, and I was greatly encouraged that he believed my story. We discussed the possibility of fighting extradition, but he felt it would be a waste of time and money because I was bound to lose. He advised me to return to North Carolina and offered to recommend an attorney there.

Shackled like an animal, I was taken to Greensboro, where Jack and Danny had implicated me in every crime they had committed. Knowing I was innocent, I felt optimistic about being freed. My new attorney was very impressive.

"If you're telling the truth, you don't have a thing to worry about," he said. He left to investigate further and returned three hours later.

"They don't have a thing on you, but they want to work a deal," he said.

In exchange for information about the men I had known at the nightclub, all charges in North Carolina (which I had not committed) would be dropped. The term for this is *nol pros*. I told everything I knew, and plans for arraignment in North Carolina were dropped.

My attorney paid me a final visit and offered to stay on the case, working out of his Charlotte office. He would bring in another noted attorney, and the two of them would work through a lawyer in Atlanta.

"For $7,000 you'll never get a day," he promised.

I was out of money, in debt, and feeling cocky.

"If I can get the money and put it in escrow, will you accept that?" I asked, knowing he would be paid only if he won the case. He agreed to the arrangement.

"I've got news for you," I grinned. "I don't have any money."

"You have a family," he suggested. My grin faded.

"Leave my family out of this! I'm willing to take my chances."

Facing the charges in Atlanta didn't really worry me. After all, I wasn't guilty. I'd be honest with the authorities, and they would understand that I wasn't a murderer. At the very worst, I'd be placed on probation. I didn't realize the authorities had spent a year building their case, and Jack and Danny had worked a deal to get a lighter sentence in return for testifying against me. The trap was laid, and I stepped into it.

I was shackled to another prisoner for the trip to Georgia in the custody of two detectives who had been told that I was extremely dangerous. They stopped at the county jail in Charlotte, North Carolina, so we could take a bathroom break—with our hands handcuffed to our waists and our feet shackled to each other. It was only one of a multitude of humiliations to come.

After a night in Atlanta's Fulton County Jail, I was taken in handcuffs on March 3, 1970, to appear before the district attorney. Because I was not represented by counsel, this was an illegal procedure. Unfortunately, I did not understand that then.

The district attorney pulled my file and said, "See this? I know everything about you. I've sent three men to the electric chair, and you will be the fourth. You will die."

That was not what I had expected to hear. I'd been led to believe he was a Christian man—an ordained minister—and that he was going to offer a deal. I'd tell everything, and he'd give me a break. I was shocked.

"I understand you have told some people in North

Carolina about your innocence," the D.A. continued. "I
don't believe it. You are a mastermind criminal." Then he
turned to the investigator who had brought me to his office.

"You know, I kind of like this man," he said, changing
his tone. "I was ready to believe he was an animal, but he's
clean cut . . . a college man. He's not what I expected."

"I'll tell you what," he said to me. "I'm offering you a
deal: twenty years if you'll plead guilty. There will be no
trial. You'll just go on down to the prison and start doing
your time. What do you say to that?"

By now I realized I was in trouble, but clearly this man
was my enemy. I was sarcastic.

"I'll take ten years and you take ten. Let's go on down
there and do it together."

"You're going to die in the electric chair!" he snarled.
"Get him out of here!"

I was taken back to my cell, and for two weeks I didn't
hear from anyone. Finally, on a Friday afternoon, I was told,
"Your attorney wants to see you." How could that be? I had
no money to hire an attorney.

A cage of metal bars separated me from the man who
identified himself as head of the public defender's
department.

"I've studied your file," he said. "They have an open-and-
shut case against you. Two men are going to testify that
you're a mastermind criminal, that you threatened their
lives, and forced them to go with you into a store with instructions to kill every person in there. They can send you
to the electric chair. I have connections with the district
attorney, and I can get you twenty years if you'll plead
guilty."

"I can see that you know nothing about me," I said in
disgust. "You believe I'm guilty."

"I *know* you're guilty," he said.

"Let me tell you something," I yelled, trying to reach
through the bars to choke him. "You're not my attorney,
and I will not plead guilty! Tell the district attorney that my

original offer stands: I'll do ten if he'll do ten, and I'm ready to go anytime *he's* ready."

"You're going to die, you sorry ---," he promised. "You're a murderer and you're going to die! I'm dropping off the case, but let me tell you something: You'll regret the day you were born."

A week later I was told to be ready at five o'clock in the morning to go for trial. I was charged with a capital offense, and I didn't even have an attorney!

After a sleepless night I was taken to a holding cell at Superior Court for hours of waiting. About 10 A.M. a guard marched me into the courtroom. I recognized the prosecutor and the public defender who had cursed me at the jail when he dropped from the case.

The first case to be announced was "Donald Harold Morris." Even my name was stated backward! The public defender spoke.

My God! What am I going to do? They're going to railroad me! I'm going to die!

The public defender walked over to me and whispered, "I can get you twenty years. Will you plead guilty?"

"I'm ready for trial, but I'll be tried for your murder. I'm going to break your neck!" I threatened.

"Your Honor, may we approach the bench?" he said. He and the prosecutor conferred briefly with the judge. The prosecutor announced that because key witnesses from South Carolina had not arrived, the case would be delayed for another month. Later that day I lay in my cell thinking.

I've made enemies . . . I can't win . . . they're going to kill me!

The jailer interrupted my thoughts.

"I have been authorized to offer you twenty years," he said. "Will you take it?"

"Authorized by whom?" I asked.

"The chief judge," he replied.

"Tell the chief judge that I'll do ten if he'll do ten, and let's get started on it today."

"You're going to die," he declared. "They're going to fry you!"

The days dragged by. On a Friday afternoon about a month later, I was told that my new attorney wanted to see me. Again I was puzzled. In the visiting room stood a well-dressed, successful-looking man who said he had been appointed by the judge to represent me. After asking several questions about the crime, he said that a trial was set for Monday.

"I've studied your brief," he said, "and I've asked for a Bill of Particulars. I know what we're facing. Two criminals are going to testify against you—a man who has never been in trouble. We'll discredit their testimony. They don't have a case."

What a relief to hear a man say that he believed in me! He thought I was innocent and that we could win the case!

On Monday morning, June 15, 1970, at 9 A.M. in Superior Court, downtown Atlanta, I went on trial for my life.

At three o'clock every morning during the trial I was taken from my cell to the courthouse to wait until the proceedings began at 9 A.M. The prosecutor had done his homework, and he ate my attorney alive. I learned that mine was a civil lawyer who had never tried a criminal case, and we made some grave errors. I intended to tell the truth and wanted to be sworn in, but my attorney objected to my taking the witness stand.

"This man is sharp, and he'll make a fool out of you," he warned.

I had told him I had no family, and we did not subpoena any character witnesses. How could we? I met the attorney on Friday, and we went to trial on Monday. He insisted that I didn't need character witnesses anyway.

"Just let them present their case, and we'll attack that. I have the last charge to the jury. They don't have a case." He was confident.

Furthermore, he said that in the state of Georgia, I could take the stand without being sworn in and say anything I wanted to say without being cross-examined. That was the greatest news I'd ever heard.

But the trial was a farce. The police officers and detectives who had investigated the shooting, the ambulance driver, and people who were at the scene all testified to establish that a murder had been committed, but none could link me to the scene of the crime.

Not until the trial did I learn the facts about the robbery. There had been twelve people in the store. The man who had been killed was the husband of one of the cashiers. A total of $590 was stolen during the robbery.

Early in the trial, Jack and Danny sent me a message by way of another inmate. They said they had made a deal, and they advised me to plead guilty for a twenty-year sentence so I would avoid the death penalty. Their concern for my future was not so evident when they took the witness stand to testify against me.

They were brought in separately, and neither looked at me except when the prosecutor asked him to point out the alleged murderer. Listening to their false testimony, I wanted to kill them. It's a good thing I didn't have a gun!

Essentially, they testified that I had planned each of a series of robberies, and had threatened their lives if they didn't help me carry out my plans. Sometime before the supermarket robbery, I had gone to the store to determine the best way to carry out the theft. I had ordered Jack and Danny to kill everyone in the store, they said.

The manager of the store and the cashier whose husband was killed were each called to the stand. They gave details of the murder, and the widow wept as she spoke. When asked if they had ever seen me before, both of them said they had not.

When the prosecutor finished presenting evidence, I took the witness stand. On the advice of my lawyer, I made an unsworn statement which would prevent the prosecuting attorney from cross-examining me. I told of my college days and stressed that I had never been in trouble. After testifying

for over an hour, I stepped down with a feeling of confidence
that I had done a very good job portraying the kind of person
I was. At the same time, I felt optimistic because none of
the eyewitnesses had ever seen me before. My nightmare
was about to end, and I was relieved.

Then it was time for the prosecutor to begin his closing
arguments. "Ladies and gentlemen of the jury," he began,
"weren't you impressed with this man? He's a college man—
well-dressed, with a stirring vocabulary. Did you notice how
he handled himself? He's not your normal criminal; he's a
mastermind!"

After reviewing all that the men had said about my supposed involvement in the Atlanta robbery and shooting, he
said I had killed other people as well. His statement should
not have been allowed because I had never been indicted
for any other crimes.

Walking over to the jury, he continued, "If this man is
what he says he is, why wouldn't he be sworn in? Any man
who will not put his hand on the Bible is a lying cheat, a
snake in the grass. Morris is a murderer! If you don't convict
him, I'll take my wife and kids and leave this town. I'd never
live near the man."

He rested his case.

The jury retired about 9 o'clock that night and at 1 A.M.
they returned, unable to reach a verdict. They asked the
judge if I could receive a lesser sentence than death, but he
refused. The jury retired for the night, and I went back to
jail. At 3 A.M. I was awakened and taken to the courthouse
to await the verdict.

At 11 A.M. on June 18, I entered the courtroom in handcuffs. When the jurors had filed in, the judge asked for the
verdict. The foreman handed it to the clerk, who gave it to
the prosecutor. A grin spread over his face as he looked at
me.

"Guilty as charged!" he declared.

The judge received the written verdict and noted that the
jury had recommended mercy, meaning that I would auto-

matically receive a life sentence instead of the death penalty. The judge said, "Donald Harold Morris . . ."

Again my first and middle names were reversed. Grasping at a straw, my attorney had filed a motion that I was illegally indicted because of the confusion over my name. The motion was denied.

Forever the words of the judge would ring in my memory.

"Young man, for the crime of armed robbery, I sentence you to hard labor at the state penitentiary for the rest of your natural life. And for the crime of murder, I sentence you to hard labor at the state penitentiary for the rest of your natural life. Take him away."

"Your Honor, I can't do it!" I cried. "There's no way that I can serve two life sentences!"

"Young man," he said, "you go to the prison and do your best."

"Wait a minute. May I say something?" I asked.

"What is it?"

"Your Honor, two days ago when I was taken from this courtroom in handcuffs and shackles, three of the jurors saw me. I request a mistrial." (The shackles indicated that I was already incarcerated and that I was considered dangerous, which would lead the jurors to an assumption of guilt.)

Angrily, he overruled the request.

Seeing that my chances were running out, I quicky added, "I would like to poll the jurors. I want each of them to look me in the eye and tell me they want me to spend the rest of my life in prison. I want them to say they did not see me in handcuffs."

"That is your right," the judge agreed. "Poll the jurors."

Each juror said that I was guilty, but not one of them looked me in the eye. Although three admitted seeing me in shackles and handcuffs, the judge held to his decision to overrule the request for mistrial. Reaching into my pocket, I pulled out an appeal that I had prepared during the night.

"Your Honor, I respectfully appeal my case and ask that I be allowed to remain in the Fulton County Jail until all of

my rights have been fully exhausted." I knew that if I could
stay there without getting a number on my back, my chances
of winning an appeal were much greater.

"You have thirty days to appeal your case," the judge
said.

Throughout the proceedings my attorney had appeared
more nervous than I. Beads of perspiration stood on his
forehead. Hearing the verdict, he cried. He said he was sorry
and promised to appeal the case. I told him that I no longer
trusted him.

The prosecutor smiled as I walked by in shackles. I
stopped in front of him.

"So you're a Christian—a preacher," I said. "I hope to
God I never get religion!"

As I walked to my cell, I passed the cell in which Jack
and Danny were being held. How I wanted to kill them! I
spit as far as I could to reinforce my promise.

"They say that I'll die here. I swear on my father's grave
that I won't! I will live to kill you both! And if I can't get
you, I'll kill your wives, your mothers, your kids. You will
die. I swear to it, you will die!"

I didn't sleep that night, knowing that down the hall were
the men who had destroyed my life.

CHAPTER 3

FULL IMPACT

The night of my conviction was one of the loneliest of my life. There had been hope until I was sentenced, but as I lay in my cell, the finality of the verdict began to soak in. Over and over I heard the words of the jury: *Guilty as charged! Guilty as charged! Guilty!*

I am guilty, I reasoned, *but not as charged. I am guilty of associating with scum, guilty of living a low life, guilty of some irresponsible choices—but not guilty of robbery and murder!*

In my mind I retried the case, remembering every word spoken on the witness stand, every facial expression, every emotional response. I had been so confident I would win. My family would never even have to know about the trial, and none of my friends back home in North Carolina would hear about it, either.

But it hadn't worked that way. I'd played a deadly game, and I had lost. Since that time I've watched the faces of many people who received the death penalty or multiple life sentences. Some tried to fight the district attorney. Some cried. Some fell to their knees. Some fainted. Some laughed at the judge. Some tried to commit suicide.

Although I made attempts to change the outcome of the trial by requesting the jury to be polled and asking for a mistrial, I hadn't raised my voice. Except for my comments to the prosecutor as I walked out of the courtroom, I had controlled my temper. I took the verdict calmly, even though

I was not prepared for it. I had even read my appeal calmly.

As the hours ticked by and the shock began to wear off, I began to realize, little by little, what the guilty verdict and the double life sentence meant. I was only twenty-nine years old, but my life was virtually over. To spend the rest of my life in prison was little more than a living death. *How could I have wasted my life like that?* I thought. *I could have made use of my opportunities to become whatever I wanted.*

Around three o'clock in the morning, the full impact hit me, and there was no stopping the tears. The only thing I could hear was the sound of my own sobbing. Darkness engulfed my soul as I remembered my mother.

She doesn't even know where I am. I'll never survive the violence of prison life. I'll die! But I don't want to die. More than ever before in my life, I want to live!

Throughout the long night I wept. *Why has this happened to me?* I kept asking myself. *Why am I here?* I tried to remember the name of the man who was killed in the robbery. I reminded myself to look in the newspaper to find out who he was. Finally, exhausted, I fell into a fitful sleep.

The next morning a guard showed me a copy of the *Atlanta Constitution*. My conviction was big news, and when the guard handed me the paper, I snapped, "You should have been there and seen it firsthand!"

As I read the account, I was astonished at the distortions. The story described a heinous murderer—a villain I could not even recognize.

That's not me! They're talking about somebody else! If only they knew me, knew who I really am . . . They're going to find out how wrong they are!

I didn't see my attorney again until after the trial. He sent a letter, stating that he had bypassed the usual channels and appealed directly to the United States Supreme Court. He had done all he could do, he said, and he wished me luck.

The days dragged by as I awaited the outcome of my appeal in a musty eight-by-ten foot cell in the Fulton County Jail. With the conviction of a felony came the loss of my

United States citizenship. Stripped of my rights, I became a ward of the state.

Once a week I was allowed out of the cell for a shower. My meals were served on a tray the guard pushed under the door. There was a tiny window in the cell, but it was too high for me to see outside. For two and a half years, I did not see the sky, the sun, the moon, the stars. It was my first encounter with solitary confinement, and each day I drifted further from my sense of humanity.

The longer I remained in the cell, the more enraged and distorted my thoughts became. Everyone was my enemy, and I even began to hate my own mother. *She knows where I am!* I thought. *She's left me here alone. Like everyone else, she has turned against me.*

My hatred and rage evolved into a seething thirst for revenge. I wanted to hurt people—to kill the prosecutor and those who testified against me. Then one day a new prisoner came to the jail, and he gave me some information that intensified my determination to get even with Jack and Danny.

The new inmate knew both of them, and he told me what had happened. The two had been sentenced to twenty years for their part in the robbery, but because of their cooperation, their sentences were commuted. The day after my trial, they walked out of jail and into freedom.

"They're bragging about how they set you up," the new prisoner told me. "It's a shame they got away with it."

I offered him all the money in my account if he would kill them for me. He promised to do it and took my money, but I never heard from him again. Still, it gave me satisfaction for a short while to think that something might have happened to my two enemies.

Day after day I paced the floor of my cell, waiting for some word about my appeal. My hatred for Jack and Danny and for the prosecutor energized me, and I began to wonder—*am I even human?* It was a question I repeated many times in the days and months that followed. My behavior certainly belied my humanity. I screamed at the guards, waving my arms at them, and I even threw filthy commode water into their faces.

That behavior landed me in a "strip cell," also known as a "slicker." Authorities claim that this tiny cell with metal walls and a concrete floor is designed to keep a prisoner from harming himself. Although its construction appears to support the idea, clearly, its purpose is total humiliation. It is an effective way to break the spirit of a man.

Usually the inmate's clothing is taken away, but this time I was allowed a shirt and a pair of pants. Because I was not considered suicidal, I was also permitted to have a bed. There was no running water, so I had to ask the guard for water when I was thirsty. I was literally reduced to begging for this necessity of life.

While I was in the slicker, an inmate in the next cell stopped up his toilet, flooding his cell and mine with human waste. As we waded through the filth that eventually became a foot deep, the guards turned water hoses on us, laughing all the while. I'll never forget their mockery of us. I threatened to kill one of them, but he continued to laugh.

I had other opportunities to witness the devastating psychological effect that slickers had on inmates. On one occasion in a cell adjoining mine, a man began hallucinating. Convinced that someone was trying to kill him, he beat his brains out on the bars. Another prisoner swallowed a long bolt he found. Another swallowed bedsprings, and others ingested knives.

When I was released from the slicker and returned to my cell, depression subdued me. I lay on my rack, lost in loneliness and despair. Occasionally I thought about asking for help, but I had too much pride. Besides, there was no one to ask. *No one cares, anyway,* I told myself. For my entire life I had felt that there was not one person on whom I could depend, and so I never cried for help.

I didn't call on God to help me, either. My thoughts traveled a different course. *There is no God,* I decided. *If he were real, he would never allow this to happen.*

For months I wavered between wanting to die and wanting to live. At some point during those endless days, I finally made up my mind to live. Then, when I had been in jail for more than two years, the Georgia Supreme Court made its decision about my appeal.

"Hey, big boy! Read this!" a guard said, slapping me on the shoulder as he handed me a newspaper clipping. I glanced at the headline:

"Georgia Supreme Court Denies Harold Donald Morris a New Trial"

My eyes blurred as I read the words. I could scarcely take it in. But the guard did not allow me time to consider the news.

"Now you *really* belong to us!" he beamed. "Today you start digging ditches!" He gloated about what the other prisoners would do to me at Georgia State Penitentiary, and I shuddered at his repulsive prophecy: "You're gonna be *raped,* Morris, 'cause you ain't tough. Get your stuff."

My "stuff" consisted of the clothes I was wearing. When I was arrested, everything I owned disappeared, and to this day I don't know what happened to my personal effects. Facing two life sentences, I didn't worry about leaving things behind.

It was a forty-mile trip to the diagnostic and classification center in Jackson, Georgia, where inmates underwent psychological and physical testing before being taken to the penitentiary.

A male social worker with long hair and a master's degree in sociology started to explain how to survive in prison. Of couse, he had never spent a day behind bars.

"Have you ever been there?" I asked.

"No," he said.

"Well, I don't want to talk to you." As I started to leave the room, he asked about my family.

"I have no family. I'm an orphan," I lied.

"You're a first offender," he noted. "I've looked at your record. There's nothing against you. You're not like the rest. Most inmates fit a pattern. You're different. You're intelli-

gent. I'm going to try to help you. I can recommend place-
ment if you'll tell me where you want to go. What's your
first choice?"

"Georgia State Penitentiary," I replied.

"That's the worst prison in the country!" he said. "No one
wants to go there. You're crazy!" He didn't realize that I
was playing games.

A man with two life sentences doesn't tell the system
where he wants to go! I knew no prisoners other than the
two men who had testified against me, and they had gotten
off scot-free. The social worker assumed that I had friends
at Georgia State Penitentiary, so he recommended another
facility. I didn't care. I was just trying to blow his mind.

When aptitude tests were given, I played games again,
deliberately giving incorrect answers. Why should I try for
high scores? I was going to die in prison. I insisted I'd been
to school only two days in my life—the first day to see what
it was like, and the second day to tell the teacher I wasn't
coming back.

After my tests were finished three months later, I was
taken to the prison van, along with a black inmate. No one
bothered to explain what was happening.

"Can you tell me where we're going?" I asked one of the
guards.

"Chatham County Prison."

Despite the nature of my "crimes" and my stiff prison
sentence, I had secretly hoped to be sent to a medium-
security facility. But Chatham County Prison was maximum-
security. That's all I knew about it.

"Where is the prison?" I asked.

"In Savannah, Georgia."

A while later the guard nudged his companion and smiled
as he turned to look at us.

"Say, can you swim?" he said. Knowing that he was being
smart, I didn't respond.

The black inmate said, "Yes, sir, I can swim."

"Good. Maybe the alligators won't get you. We're gonna

have both of you digging ditches. You'll be in water up to your neck. If we don't kill you, the alligators will."

When I kept silent, he said, "Has the cat got your tongue?" Still I didn't reply.

"Old big boy is pretty tough," he said. "But I'm gonna tell you something, city slicker. You're ours forever, and we're gonna break you."

Unable to take the abuse any longer, I said, "Let me tell you something, punk. You'll never break me. You're not man enough to break me!"

Chatham County Prison was a dilapidated facility with two large dormitories housing about 200 men with another fifty inmates in smaller dorms. I was assigned to one of the large buildings equipped with two commodes, two sinks, and one shower for ninety-eight men. I was one of only four white inmates in the building.

While I was in the shower, someone stole my glasses. I asked the house man—the inmate in charge of keeping the dorm clean—if he knew anything about them. He hadn't seen them.

"Everybody give me your attention," I yelled. "My glasses are missing. If you see them, please bring them to me. I need them." I lay on the bed wondering what I should do next. Finally I stood and said, "Listen to me. If I catch the man who stole my glasses, I'll kill him. I don't want any trouble, but the man who stole my glasses deserves to die. I just want you to know that." I lay down again.

About an hour later the house man whispered, "I know who took your glasses, but you can't let him know I told. It was that Black Muslim over there."

I walked over to the man and asked, "Did you get my glasses?" He didn't answer.

"I believe you took them, and I'm going to give you five minutes to return them. If you don't, I'm going to kill you."

He jumped up and ran to the door, screaming, "Let me out! That man's gone crazy!"

The guards took him out and returned to punish me. After

I explained what happened, they questioned the inmate. He admitted hiding my glasses atop a heater. The guards laughed as they handed me what was left of the lenses and melted frames.

About two hours later four black inmates walked over to my bunk.

"Do you think you're bad?" one said.

"I'm not bad. I have two life sentences, and I'm just starting out. My fight is not with you. That man stole my glasses. I don't steal, and any man who steals from me is going to pay. I don't want any trouble, but I'm not afraid of you. That's the way it is." He thought about what I'd said.

Then he replied, "You're all right," and shook my hand. He turned to walk away, and the others followed. I nearly had a heart attack.

The classification committee informed me that I would be digging ditches outside the prison grounds and asked if I had any physical problems. I had gained a great deal of weight during the two-and-a-half years that I'd been locked up, and I explained that I did not feel physically able to dig ditches. They responded with some choice words and warned me that I would be punished if I didn't report for work the next day.

When morning came I refused to work until a doctor examined a knot that I had discovered on my back.

"You'd better hope there is something wrong with you," the guard growled. "If the doctor doesn't find anything, you'll go to the hole for fourteen days." The hole was the ultimate in prison punishment—solitary confinement in total darkness with one bread-and-water meal a day.

I pulled up my shirt and showed the knot to the doctor, but he never touched it.

"There's nothing wrong with you," he said, making a note on his report that I was able to work.

For violations within the prison, inmates were tried by a kangaroo court composed of several guards and a counselor. Most of the counselors were former guards with no professional training in counseling. Knowing the court would sentence me to the hole for refusing to work, I asked to see the warden, but he wouldn't be in until the next day. When morning came I again refused to work; the court sentenced me to twenty-eight days in the hole.

"I want to appeal this to the warden," I persisted. No one had ever done that, and the guards didn't know what to do. I was allowed to return to the dorm to wait until the warden could see me.

I explained to the warden, "Sir, you don't know me very well, but I have two life sentences. I'll probably die in prison. I realize that you didn't put me here. You're not the enemy, and I have no animosity toward you. I'm well-educated and willing to work, but I can't dig ditches. I don't want to be out in public. It's humiliating. I'll work at the prison typing, washing clothes, anything!"

"We only have inside jobs for a few men," he said. "You'll have to work outside the facility like everybody else."

"I won't! I'd rather die! Please listen to me," I pleaded. "If you put me back on detail, I'll either kill a guard, or he'll kill me. Either way you lose your job. You don't want that. Send me to Georgia State Penitentiary. At least there I won't be out in public."

"You're the only man I've ever met who wanted to be sent to the State Penitentiary," he said. "Are you crazy?" He finally agreed to the transfer but insisted that I go to the hole until arrangements could be made, probably a week to ten days.

Life at the jail had been so bad that I couldn't imagine spending ten days totally alone in complete darkness. Digging ditches sounded awful, but at least there would be light, and I could *see* other people.

"All right," I conceded. "Let me dig ditches until then. I won't cause any problems."

The warden agreed, and six days later a guard came to my cell at 5 A.M. As he led me out past sleeping inmates, he said in a puzzled tone, "You're either the bravest man who has ever been in this prison, or you're a fool."

With my hands handcuffed to my waist and my ankles in shackles, I climbed into the old prison van with two guards who appeared to be close to seventy years of age. They offered no harassment during the trip to the Georgia State Penitentiary, seventy-five miles northwest of Savannah. It was December 6, 1971, and the gray winter morning reflected the gloom in my soul. During the ride, I had plenty of time to think about the events that had led to my incarceration.

CHAPTER 4

SHATTERED DREAMS

Although I had chosen the playboy lifestyle for myself, I had not been proud of it. To keep my family from knowing about my drinking and girl chasing, I had deliberately lost contact with them. No one back home—not even my mother—had any idea where I was now. I was glad of that, but the mere thought of my family sent my mind flashing back through my early years.

Georgetown, South Carolina, was a small, friendly town of 15,000 people on the Atlantic coast. As a child, I was fascinated that many of the stores along Front Street were built over the water, and fishing boats could ease right up to the rear of the buildings to unload the day's catch. I never thought life could be better than it was in Georgetown during my early years.

My father worked at the International Paper Company's mill, one of the largest of its kind in the world. He was a middle-aged widower with seven children when he met and married my mother, and she was twenty-one years younger than he. Four more of us came along after they were married; I was second-to-last.

Life in Georgetown must have been tough with so many mouths to feed, and my father longed to return to the farming life he had known as a boy. By the time I was in third grade, Dad finally left his job at the mill and moved us to the country. We settled on a farm at Pleasant Hill, South Carolina, about forty miles from Georgetown. It was a sparsely populated community with fields as far as the eye could see. The pace was so slow and the community so small, there wasn't even a traffic light.

Times were hard, and it was difficult to make a living off the land as sharecroppers. We often didn't know where our next meal was coming from, and to help make ends meet, Mom took a job at the International Paper Company's container division back in Georgetown. A neighbor provided the transportation.

Looking back, I don't know how my mother managed to meet the needs of eleven children, help with the chores on the farm, and work in Georgetown, too. She seemed tireless, and I always thought she was the sweetest woman on earth. A gentle lady who always looked for the best in people, she was loved and respected by everyone who knew her. Even-tempered and generous, she never turned a stranger away without giving him a hot meal. There was something different about her, but I couldn't name what that difference was.

On rare occasions when she could slip out of the house without my father knowing, she attended church services. Once or twice my father went with her, and I even went a few times to see my friends, to meet girls, or to attend social functions. I was interested in having fun when I got away from the farm—nothing else.

Although my father had little use for church activities, he was a good man who expected goodness in return, an honest man who demanded honesty from his family and from those with whom he did business. He loved to tell salty stories, and my friends often came to hear the earthy experiences of his boyhood and the outlandish yarns born of his imagination. He also had a huge storehouse of off-color jokes. In spite of his raunchy language, his engaging personality seemed to win over anyone who knew him.

Because my father had lots of common sense and could hold his own in a conversation, people assumed he had been well-educated. No one ever guessed that he couldn't write his own name and that he hadn't been to school a day in his life. Because he was so honest, Dad never tried to hide his

lack of education. But whenever the conversation was turned
to education, I changed the subject. Although I was proud
of my father in many ways, his illiteracy humiliated me.

Nevertheless, I hated school, and I'd never have gone a
single day if my father had not insisted. "You'd better make
good grades," he warned me. "I don't want you to end up
like me." He desperately wanted me to have an education,
but paradoxically, he did not know how to encourage me.
Many times he kept me out of school to work on the farm.
If I wanted to play a game of baseball in the afternoon, I
had to stay home from school in the morning to finish my
chores. Work always came first.

Every day after school, every weekend, every summer, I
worked on the farm until dark—and sometimes long after
dark—cropping tobacco, picking cotton, and feeding the
cows. I plowed with mules until we could afford a tractor.
There was little else in our life, outside the farm.

Good times were few, other than an occasional swim in
the lake or the annual trip to Hemingway when the fair came
to town. We couldn't afford a television set, and keeping
the chores caught up left little time to cultivate friendships.
Our nearest neighbor lived a mile away, so my brother Carl,
who was a year and ten months older than I, was my best
friend.

There was one thing my father enjoyed more than working
the farm, and that was hunting. I hated the overnight hunting
trips because my dad couldn't understand how much the
killing bothered me. I simply could not kill an animal. Whenever my dad positioned me on a deer stand, I desperately
hoped a deer wouldn't come. I knew I could never pull the
trigger. As I grew older, I refused to go along on the hunting
trips.

Often on those trips he drank heavily, and many times I
saw him pass out in a drunken stupor. One day he returned
from a trip feeling ill after skinning a deer. Flinging his beer
can across the yard, he declared he would never take another
drink. As far as I know, he never drank again.

Although the people in the community admired this kind

of determination and fortitude in my father, at home his strong will made him hard, domineering, and determined to have his own way. I loved him deeply, but I did not know how to express that love, and neither did he. Our inability to communicate was complicated by the great gap between our ages—he was forty-eight when I was born. He could not understand why I disliked school and why I hated hunting and killing animals. Because we never understood each other, we never developed a close relationship.

Because my father was so unbending about what he wanted, he demanded obedience. And when we *didn't* obey, his discipline was both swift and harsh. Using a board or a belt, he would beat me. "You're no good!" he would rage at me. You'll never amount to anything!"

No matter how bruised and battered I was after a beating, the verbal abuse was more painful. I told myself he didn't really mean it, but his words etched themselves upon my soul, and I could not forget them.

But my dad was not the only one who berated me like that. At school my teachers and coaches reinforced what my father was screaming at me when I was home. "You're no good, Morris," they would say. "You'll end up being a no-account."

I didn't want to believe them. High-strung, angry, and aggressive, I was determined to prove all of them wrong, bent on showing everybody that Harold Morris was worth something. To me, there was only one way to do it, and that was to become a great athlete. I wanted to be like my idol, Mickey Mantle of the New York Yankees.

My brother Carl also loved baseball. Strong and athletic, he was a left-handed pitcher. He spent hours pitching to me, and that practice worked to my advantage.

Although Pleasant Hill was one of the smallest schools in the state (the junior high and senior high grades were combined), we had a baseball and a basketball team. Since the students were from farm families who valued hard work as highly as my father did, chores always came ahead of sports.

One day when I was in seventh grade, the high school baseball coach called me out of class. His catcher had to help harvest his father's tobacco crop, and the coach wondered if I could serve as a substitute.

The catcher's gear weighed more than I did, but I caught a great game, called the signals, and even got two hits. The local newspaper carried a story, calling me the hitting star of the game! For the rest of the season and for the next year as well, I caught for Carl whenever he pitched. By the time I was a freshman, I was starting catcher.

All during that time, I longed to play sports at a more competitive level. Often as I plowed the fields, I'd see a school bus with *Big Red Winyah Gators* painted on the side. It was carrying Winyah's athletic teams to games. Winyah High School in Georgetown had a great sports tradition. The teams wore beautiful red and white uniforms, and the newspaper gave their games generous coverage. In 1954 Winyah was the number one high school in the nation.

One autumn day, I stopped the tractor and watched the bus fade into the distance. The sun was setting through the trees, and only the wind and earth heard my dream. *I'd give anything to be a Winyah Gator—to dress in one of those red and white uniforms. If only I could play at Winyah High!*

Then one day my dreams began to come true. For whatever reasons, Dad decided it was time to give up farming and move back to Georgetown. It would take a while to sell the equipment, but Dad said I could stay in Georgetown with one of my brothers and go to school at Winyah. I was thrilled! For me, moving from the sticks to a town of 15,000 was like going to New York City.

As much as I wanted to go to school at Winyah High, I was scared to death. It was a big school, and I was a bashful country boy. I didn't know how to "act," and I had a tremendous longing to be accepted and loved. In almost every area, I felt inadequate—but in sports, I knew I could be a winner. Natural athletic ability and my six-foot-two-inch, 180-pound frame gave me confidence and an advantage in athletics. For the first time in my life, I knew I was good at something.

Winyah's football games were the biggest events in town, and the first game I ever saw dazzled me. Mesmerized, I marveled as the quarterback, wearing number 50, scored one touchdown after another. The fans cheered, whistled, and screamed their support and approval.

"I'm going to play football next year," I said to a friend.

He laughed, "You don't know anything about football!"

"Oh, yes I do," I lied. "I'm good—and next year, I'm going to play."

I didn't know what "first and ten" meant, but I knew this: I'd play football for Winyah High, and I'd wear number 50.

When I went out for football in my junior year, I knew so little about the game that the coach asked me if I'd ever played before. I admitted that I hadn't.

"Boy, you *are* country!" he said. Everybody laughed, and the nickname "Country" stayed with me all through high school and later years. I hated it.

At our first scrimmage the coach assigned me to a defense position until another player broke his arm during the first quarter. For the rest of the game—and for the season and throughout the next year—I played both defense and offense, rarely missing a down.

But I didn't limit myself to football. When I asked the basketball coach about trying out for the varsity team, he laughed. "All right," he finally said, "It's another month until practice starts, and some of the players come here at night to get in shape. You can work out with them, and then we'll see."

I was scared. *What if I'm not good enough after all?* Although I hadn't learned the fundamentals of the game, I could shoot a basketball, and apparently I made a good impression. The coach not only picked me for varsity, but he also started me in the first game.

Being one of the top players thrilled me, especially since our first game was against Pleasant Hill. I scored thirteen points. The game was more than a victory for our team; it established me as an athlete, and that recognition was my key to peer acceptance throughout high school. It gave my self-esteem a tremendous boost.

I loved all sports, but baseball was special. Bad grades cost me my position in my sophomore year, and during my junior year, I was suspended from the team for three games for being late to school. During one of those games a scout for the Cleveland Indians came and asked for me. The coach told him I'd been kicked off the team. Later, the coach could hardly wait to tell me I'd blown my big chance; the scout had decided I wasn't the kind of material he needed. I realized I'd missed the scout because I'd ignored the rules. My heart was broken. Time after time, that happened in my life: I always seemed to mess up the big opportunity.

Nevertheless, the goals that I set upon entering Winyah High became a reality. During my senior year I served as captain of the basketball, baseball, and football teams. I felt an enormous sense of accomplishment when I was recognized as best athlete in the school, and I enjoyed the attention the girls gave me.

One especially beautiful girl, Katie, had captured my attention in my junior year. Her numerous beauty titles verified my opinion that she was absolutely gorgeous. The only child of wealthy, college-educated parents, Katie knew exactly where she was going in life. A straight-A student, very goal-oriented and emotionally sound, she was exactly the opposite of me, and I was ecstatic when she agreed to go steady with me. Although we loved each other, we agreed to break up when she graduated and went away to college.

I missed Katie, but I filled that void by going to parties with other girls, and I ran with a loose crowd of older guys. My two closest friends were a couple of years older than I. One boy had a fine character and a positive influence on me, but I was attracted to the wild ways of my other friend, and it was with him that I drank my first beer. Easily swayed by peer pressure, I submitted to the standards of the older crowd to gain acceptance.

Yet in spite of my athletic accomplishments and the ap-

proval of my friends, something was missing. I never truly
saw myself as successful. Perhaps it was because the person
who mattered the most to me could not understand me. Day
after day my father tried to discourage me from participating
in athletics.

"You're wasting your time," he would say to me. "You
need to quit playing games all the time and do something
worthwhile in your life. If you don't, you'll end up being a
good-for-nothing!" Not having any background in sports, he
could not appreciate my ability, and he steadfastly refused
to attend any of my games.

During my senior year, the homecoming football game
was Father-Son Night. The players' fathers were to sit together at the fifty-yard line, and at halftime they would be
introduced, along with their sons. I begged my dad to go.

"It's a very special night, and all of the fathers will be
there," I said. "I'm captain of the team, and it would mean
a lot to me if you would go."

Dad had never seen me play, but he finally agreed to
attend the game. As I dressed, I was beside myself with
excitement. *Tonight my dad will be on the sidelines with the
other fathers,* I thought. *Tonight he'll see how well I play,
and he'll be proud of me.* During our warm-up I ran close
to him and caught a pass, hoping he would see me. We won
the game, and I could hardly wait to hear what he would
say about my touchdown, but I didn't see him after the game.
When I got home, my father told me he had left early. I
swallowed hard and turned away.

"That's the biggest bunch of nonsense I've ever seen," he
said. "Running around wearing all that junk. You looked
like something from Mars. I couldn't tell one person from
another!"

He hadn't even recognized me! He wasn't proud of me
after all. He'd thought I looked ridiculous, and he'd walked
out. Although I realized he didn't understand the game, I
couldn't comprehend why he didn't want to be there to support me, to be proud of me—to love me.

Later that same year, another incident solidified my sense of isolation. I was chosen to play in the Coaches' All-Star Basketball Game at the University of South Carolina, and I was elated. The celebrated event was a sellout, and the fieldhouse was packed. I was chosen as one of the five starting players, and I played most of the game.

After the game, parents were hugging their sons and telling them how proud they were. I stood off to the side and tried to look inconspicuous, because none of my family or friends had come to see me play. I'd have given anything if someone had been cheering for me.

A number of college recruiters approached me after the game, offering me athletic scholarships. As much as I wanted to further my athletic career, my scholastic record worked against me. I had no choice but to reject the offers. Again, I paid the price for not applying myself in the classroom.

I knew I could not be a jock for the rest of my life, and deep inside I really wanted to be a success. The trouble was, I didn't know how. I had grown up without learning the importance of continuous goal-setting, and of moving the target higher each time the goal is reached. So, I had no plans for after my graduation, and the foundation for my future seemed to be in the fast-and-loose lifestyle I'd begun to enjoy with some of the older kids. At the time, drinking beer, chasing girls and running with an older crowd seemed to be a good way to prove myself. In reality, that lifestyle was setting the pace for days to come.

After graduation in 1958, I went to work in South Carolina National Bank's transit department, and a year later I accepted a job with the International Paper Company. By this time Katie was in her junior year at the University of South Carolina, where she was studying for a career in medical technology. While she was home for Christmas, she came to see me. She said she still loved me and had never loved anyone else. I said, "Show me you love me. Marry me."

Although Katie was a Christian and she knew I did not believe in God, she accepted my hasty proposal on two conditions: I was to take her to church, and I was never to drink. I promised. We agreed that our families shouldn't know about the marriage until she finished school, and a month later, we eloped.

Katie returned to her studies, and for nineteen consecutive weekends I drove 135 miles to Columbia to spend the night with my wife in a motel. The routine was interrupted when I began six months of National Guard training at Fort Jackson, South Carolina.

Again, athletics smoothed the way for me. Assigned to Special Services, I was chosen for the football and basketball teams, helping both teams win the Fort Jackson championship. As a reward, the players received weekend passes. Instead of going to see Katie, I spent the time drinking.

In the spring of 1961, Katie was graduated from the University of South Carolina. We made our marriage public and started housekeeping in Greensboro, North Carolina, where Katie entered a hospital program to study medical technology. At her encouragement, I gave college a try. Guilford College accepted me (I was on academic probation because of my poor high school grades), and I chose economics as a major. Between classes I did housework and hated every minute of it.

To enliven things, I joined a basketball team in an industrial league. But Katie detested sports and refused to go to my games. When I was offered an athletic scholarship at the college, she insisted that I turn it down.

Marriage hadn't been too bad when Katie and I lived apart. Now that we were together, I found myself growing tired of her and wanting to be free to sow some wild oats. Instead of talking with her about my feelings, I began staying out late with my buddies from school. I started drinking more and more, and I stopped going to church.

Katie asked the pastor to see me, and he quizzed me about my drinking. He even opened the refrigerator, looking for beer. I resented that and jumped on Katie about it. Realizing our marriage was in serious trouble, Katie did everything she could to save it. She even violated her own convictions, and agreed to drink and go to parties with me.

Katie finished her training and took a position at the hospital. I still had no goals for the future, so I dropped out of college during my senior year and found a job with a clothing company. When Katie learned about it, we separated. Yet, Katie really cared about me, and asked for a reconciliation. She tried her best to make our marriage work, but I was unwilling to be as committed to her as she was to me.

One day as Katie arrived home from work I announced, "I've packed my car. I'm leaving. I don't love you anymore."

For a moment she just stood there, as though she were stunned. When I turned toward the door, she grabbed several of my sports trophies and smashed them to the floor. I was infuriated.

"Now I hate you!" I shouted, storming out the door.

Katie filed for a legal separation when I did not return, and then she moved to California. I didn't see her again for more than a year. During that time my dad died of cancer, and with him died my last hope of having his approval. It seemed everyone had abandoned me. One night when I was drunk, I called Katie and asked her to take me back.

"Harold," she said, "if I knew you meant business and could change, I'd come back. But you'll *never* change." We didn't talk again until July of 1967, when she called to say she was coming to finalize our divorce. I let her use my car while she was in town.

After the divorce was settled, she came by my apartment and asked me to drive her to the airport. There was a bikini-clad girl of nineteen with me, but when I compared her to Katie, I realized once again that Katie was the most beautiful woman I'd ever seen. She smiled at me and said, "Well, you're a free man now. Are you happy?"

"Yes, I am," I lied.

On the way to the airport, Katie told me she would always love me and that she regretted our marriage had failed. She repeated her view of me: "If I thought you could change and be the man I once thought you were, I'd remarry you. But you have very serious problems. You'll *never* change, Harold. I'm sorry."

I watched her walk up the ramp. Both of us were crying. She turned to me and waved, then stepped into the plane and out of my life forever.

I never told my family about the divorce, and from that point on, my life went downhill fast.

CHAPTER 5

THE WHITE ELEPHANT

"Welcome to Georgia State Penitentiary." The sign at the entrance made an ironic attempt at a warm greeting. I had heard frightening stories about that massive place housing thousands of inmates who had committed every crime conceivable to man. It was known in the prison system as the "white elephant" because all the buildings were painted white. Somewhere within those formidable walls was death row, where condemned men waited for the end. The main building resembled a huge motel standing four stories high.

From a tower, a guard armed with a high-powered rifle directed us inside. Hobbling in duck-fashion because of the shackles, I stopped for a moment just inside the gate.

"Young man, how much time do you have?" asked one of the guards who had brought me from Chatham County Prison.

"Two life sentences," I answered.

"How much time have you done?" he probed.

"I'm just starting out."

His wrinkled face held a sympathetic look and his voice was solemn. "Young man, take a good look at the front door of the prison, because you will die here. You will never be free again."

The old man wasn't trying to give me a hard time; he was simply stating a fact. I didn't doubt his tragic statement. He was merely repeating the words my father, my teachers, and my wife had said: *You're no good. You'll never change. You'll never amount to anything. You will die here. You will die here. You will die. . . .*

I stood at the prison door breathing deeply the fresh air, trying to memorize the beauty of the trees and sky. I turned to look behind me. There was no one to say, "I love you." No one to say, "I care." It was the first day of the most horrible years of my life.

In the final stripping of my dignity, my head was shaved and my body sprayed for lice, a routine procedure for all inmates arriving at the prison. I was issued a pair of coveralls and a new identity—number 62345.

Additional clothes were issued—three pairs of white socks that were made at the prison; three sets of underwear stamped with the numbers of three inmates who had worn them previously; a pair of boots; and three sets of coveralls, white with blue stripes down the side. "State Prison" was stamped in black letters on the pants and the back of the shirt, along with my number.

To add to my humiliation, the inmate who issued the clothing gave me size forty underpants (I wore a thirty-three) and an extra-large T-shirt. Everybody laughed at the "green-horn." I was fresh meat.

New arrivals were detained for six weeks to three months in quarantine in M-building to determine if they could live in the general inmate population. There were three tiers of twenty cells each, with one man to a cell. The place was also called the catch-out building, where inmates were taken for protection if their lives had been threatened within the prison. Inmates who were repeatedly sentenced to the hole were sometimes placed in M-building permanently. I met men who had spent years there, but I found it to be un-bearable isolation. I was allowed out of the cell once a week for a shower, and I received my meals on a tray that was slipped under the door.

After eight weeks, I was assigned to dormitory G-3 where

115 men shared two commodes and one shower. The filth was intolerable. We slept on cots stacked in triple decks. The responsibility for assigning bunks fell to the house man, an inmate who became known as Latcheye after a prison stabbing had left one of his eyes drooping half-closed.

"If you've got any money, I'll give you a bunk on the bottom," Latcheye said. "If you don't have money, you go on top."

I couldn't believe it—a man with two life sentences, doomed to die in prison, paying for a bunk to sleep in!

"You're crazy!" I said. "I'm not paying you anything."

"Well, you get on top," he said with satisfaction.

It had been so long since I'd shaved and showered that I couldn't stand my own stinking odor. I asked Latcheye to let me borrow a towel and razor.

"I'm not giving you anything," he barked.

Nearby, an old man was busy lacing leather wallets. He looked up and spoke. "Young man, you can borrow my towel and razor."

Surprised by his kindness, I turned to him. "I appreciate that," I said. "I'll gladly repay you."

"Hey, you don't associate with people like that," Latcheye interrupted. "That man is a baby raper. He's the scum of the earth."

"I don't think I know you," I said to Latcheye.

"No, but I know you," he replied. "I've already pulled your file. You're somebody. You're a murderer."

I was dumbfounded! Accepted because I supposedly had killed someone! The prison seemed to have a kind of social hierarchy, with murderers receiving more "respect" than many of the other criminals. Thrust together in that filthy prison were killers, robbers, rapists, and homosexuals— 3,200 of the worst of Georgia's 16,000 prisoners. One man had killed his entire family. Another had buried a girl alive. One inmate was accused of raping 150 women. Lowest in this pathological caste system were "baby rapers"—the child molesters. I soon realized that a strong person puts no trust in baby rapers, bank robbers, and murderers.

Although I'd been convicted of murder, I knew my conviction was not enough to protect me from danger and assault. Inmates jostled for power, and survival became a daily challenge. There wasn't a doubt in my mind that I'd be killed. I wasn't tough enough or smart enough to survive. Desperate and miserable, I stayed to myself, speaking as little as possible, hoping that everyone would think I was tough while inside I was frightened to death. It was the loneliest kind of life.

As I learned my way around, I discovered there was a convict code, an unwritten set of rules governing behavior behind bars. An inmate who violated the code could expect harassment from inmates as well as guards.

The prison was dominated by a handful of inmates who had built a reputation for toughness. They controlled everything in the prison, including the television, which blared constantly. It was close to my bunk, but I didn't dare adjust it. Only the tough guys known as "tush hogs" were allowed to do that. On Saturdays about fifty smoking and tobacco-chewing inmates huddled around my bunk to watch cartoons. That nearly drove me out of my mind.

It had been years since I'd watched a ball game, and I was desperate to see one. As I headed to lunch one Saturday, I gathered my courage and said, "Fellas, Kentucky plays Tennessee in basketball at one o'clock today, and I'd like to watch the game. You know, we're all in here together. I want you to know I'd really like to see that game."

"We don't watch sports in here," an inmate said gruffly, adding, "I don't know who you think you are, but you ain't watching nothing on that television."

I wished I'd never mentioned it. But now that the issue was raised, it had to be settled.

"Let me tell you something," I said. "This is as much my home as it is yours. I haven't touched that television, but

I'm telling you that at one o'clock I will watch that basketball game." I turned and walked out.

When I returned from lunch, no one spoke. I leaned against the wall, afraid to turn my back to anyone. An inmate walked up to me.

"You don't know who you're messing with," he said. "Nobody comes in here and says things like that. Those guys will cut your head off. You challenged them, and if you back down, you're finished. You'll be a nobody. They'll rape you and steal everything you've got. Do you understand?" I didn't answer.

"Do you have a knife?" he asked.

"Man, I don't have anything!" I said, feeling the grip of fear.

"There's a magazine under my bed, and in the magazine is a shank," he said. A shank is a homemade knife long enough to almost pierce through a man.

"After I walk out, go over to my bed and pick up the magazine. Walk back to your bunk and act as if you're reading. If there's any trouble, you'll have a weapon."

I did exactly as he said. If his warning hadn't frightened me, the touch of that razor-sharp blade certainly did. What if I had to use it? Never before had I faced anything like this. I'd started something, and I had to go through with it. Time crawled.

At one o'clock an old western movie was playing. With the magazine in one hand, I walked over to the set and turned the channel to the ball game.

"You touch that television again and I'll kill you!" warned an inmate as he switched back to the movie.

"Fellas," I tried again, "can't we work this out? I live here, too, and I should be allowed to watch one program. I don't want any trouble, but I'm going to watch the basketball game. When it's over you can watch anything you choose for the rest of the day. That's the way it should be. I hope we can get along."

"You touch that television and you're going to hell!" The voice came from a bunk where one of the tough guys lay with his young boy lover. I knew the man's reputation—extremely dangerous. The other inmates wanted him to take up the fight.

"My fight is not with you," I said. "I don't even know you, but I've watched you turn the channel. It's only fair I have the same privilege. I don't want any trouble, but I'm ready to go to hell, if that's what it takes." I waited through an interminable silence, my body tense and drenched with sweat. Finally he spoke.

"You're the only man in this place who has any guts. I like you. What you're saying makes sense. As far as I'm concerned, you can watch anything you want." He turned his attention to the boy lying with him in the bunk.

"I'd like for you guys to watch the ball game with me," I said, changing channels again. Still grasping the magazine with the shank carefully concealed, I sat on a stool without turning my back. The inmates began walking away, disgruntled and mumbling. Only one stayed to watch the game with me.

A strange thing happened that day. Through a challenge made in ignorance and innocence, I gained respect. Knowing nothing about me, the other inmates gathered the impression that I was dangerous. If I had backed down, they would have persecuted me. It was a terrifying introduction to the law of the jungle—win, or you're through.

The prison reservation encompassed 10,000 acres of farmland with a large dairy, a hog farm, and several thousand chickens. All the work at the institution was done by inmates, laboring under the blistering Georgia sun and the watchful eyes of shotgun-carrying guards. Every two hours—wherever we were, night or day—we were counted.

Lights went out at 10 P.M. Usually I was up at 5 A.M., but this depended on one's job. Inmate cooks began baking about 1 A.M. in order to open the chow line at 5 o'clock.

Feeding 3,200 men took quite a while. We were allowed only the food that was served on our plate. Stealing a biscuit was punishable by fourteen days in the hole.

In effect, even the slightest infraction could land you in the hole. Take for example an inmate who worked in the chicken yard. He became known as Chicken Yard Shorty. One day as Chicken Yard gathered eggs, a hen jumped on him and spurred. Angrily, Chicken Yard threatened to kill the chicken if it attacked him again. The next day, the chicken jumped him once more, and Chicken Yard hit it with a stick. A guard witnessed the skirmish, grabbed Chicken Yard, and ordered him into the building where I worked as clerk.

"I'm bringing charges against this inmate," he said. That meant he would be tried in kangaroo court.

"What are the charges?" I asked.

"Murdering a chicken."

"Wait a minute. The chicken didn't die when I hit it," corrected Chicken Yard. After he wounded it, some other inmates killed the chicken and ate it.

"Change that charge to assault on a chicken," the guard said.

In court the next day, the drama unfolded.

"You have been charged with assault on a chicken. How do you plead?"

"I didn't kill the chicken," said Chicken Yard.

"How do you plead?"

"Not guilty."

"Wait outside."

When the voting concluded, Chicken Yard was brought back in.

"You have been found guilty of assault on a chicken. We sentence you to fourteen days of solitary confinement in the hole and ninety days probation. If you ever hit a chicken again, we're going to throw the book at you."

Chicken Yard exclaimed, "Praise the Lord that chicken didn't die! I would have gone to the electric chair!"

Fourteen days later, Chicken Yard Shorty came out of the hole filthy and starving. As he walked past, I cried realizing what the system had done to him. I never understood how the punishment fit the crime.

Except for the hours spent working and eating, we were locked in our cells. I hated being locked in—especially over holidays. On weekends we had yard call, where exercise was provided through intramural games. This privilege was canceled during riots or other periods of violence. Visitors were allowed on weekends and holidays, and occasionally model prisoners were allowed to make a five-minute phone call. That didn't interest me. My family and friends didn't know where I was, and I never intended to tell them.

Roaches, ants, and flies outnumbered the inmates. Once, I laid a pack of cookies on a little table in front of my bed for a snack while watching television. When I reached for a cookie, something crawled over my hand. In a matter of seconds, hundreds of ants covered the cookies.

Eventually I formed friendships with the roaches. When I arrived at the prison, I stomped them. After six months I accepted them, and as time went by I befriended them. I even named them; Homer was my favorite. I fed bread crumbs to them and played with them, holding a string for them to climb. I never killed another roach. Whenever one died in my cell it was of old age.

After I received a Bible, roaches ate the leather corners and nibbled the pages. Since we shared the same cell, I was comforted thinking that at least they were spiritual roaches!

I was not so compassionate with other insects. Killing flies was a game. I set a goal to kill 1,000 a day, marking my progress on a chart. Whenver time was running out, I'd rush to mess hall to finish my quota. One day I finished in fifteen minutes, which says something about the filth.

While looking through some files, an officer came across my chart, flies, 992; spiders, 3; miscellaneous, 6.

"What is this?" he asked. After hearing my explanation,

he roared, "Good grief! Is that what you do with your time? You're crazy!"

I found the games to be healthful thinking. They kept my mind off my mother and family. They helped me survive.

Still there was the fear that I *wouldn't* survive. I went to bed every night afraid that I would be stabbed while I slept.

One night, I lay on my bunk stripped to my underwear, yet unable to sleep in the smothering heat. The cell was black as pitch, and the only sound I heard was the snoring of my cellmate in a bunk eighteen inches away. Suddenly something struck my chest. I jumped out of bed, shouting and swinging in the dark, certain that I was going to be stabbed.

By the time I found the light, my buddy was sitting up in bed scared to death. On my bunk lay the assailant—a roach measuring at least two inches long. Our cell on the top floor of the prison was a convenient entrance for the roaches that bred on the roof. That old boy had crawled through the window, started making his way across the ceiling, and lost his grip just above me.

He stared at me while I thought of things he would say if he could talk. *Look at the big galoot. Imagine a guy that big being so frightened of me! You're really tough, Morris. You're really tough!*

I pushed him off the bed, being careful not to hurt him. Prison was that kind of place—full of filth and fear.

Nevertheless, I took pride in keeping my cell as clean as possible, and each time I was moved I had to start over. I immediately scrubbed the cell as well as I could, using toilet paper and water. Once, I bribed a guard to smuggle in some paint. He brought a little at a time, never much of one color. I painted the bunk black, the floor gray, the commode red, the wall five different colors.

"Your cell looks better than my home," the guard said.

"I'll trade with you," I offered.

After a while, the classification committee finished reviewing my file to determine the kind of work for which I was suited.

"What did you do on the outside?" a guard asked.

"I was an airplane pilot."

"Hey, we've got a smart aleck," he said. "We don't have any planes, but we've got 10,000 acres of farmland. You're going to pick peas. We're going to break you."

His plans took an unexpected turn, however, when the hospital administrator learned I could type. He needed a clerk-typist and requested that I be given the job. I was taken from the room while the matter was discussed. When I returned the guard said, "This is highly unusual. Everybody works in the fields for six months before coming inside, but we need you for this job. We'll give you a chance. You'll work on the hospital floor as a clerk-typist. But the minute you mess up, you'll be in the fields forever."

The cell assigned to me on the hospital floor housed nine men. Clearly, I would need a way to defend myself if violence broke out. Then I noticed a bucket with a mop wringer—a metal bar used to squeeze the mop. It measured nearly three feet long and was attached at the bottom of the bucket with a nut and bolt. During the night, while everybody was asleep, I removed the nut and bolt and refastened the bar with a small piece of wire I found in the cell. I could still squeeze the mop, but by yanking away the wire, I'd have a deadly weapon within seconds.

One day a young man with a cast on his arm went berserk and lunged at me in a violent attack that left both of us a bloody mess. He beat me in the head until my nose was broken. I wrestled him down and smashed his face on my knee, but neither of us was winning the fight. When I finally let him up, the inmate ran to his bed and pulled out a pair of sharp-pointed scissors.

"Now you die!" he screamed.

I had no time to reason with him, and I knew there was no way out. I'd never deliberately hurt anyone before, but

I knew this was a matter of survival. If I didn't kill him, he would kill me. I grabbed the mop wringer and started beating him. Blood blinded me, and I kept wiping it away, but I couldn't stop its flow as I battled for my life. I didn't want to kill him, and I was relieved when he went into shock. Besides a concussion, he had several broken ribs, and both arms were broken. After he was taken for treatment, the guards beat me and threw me in the hole without offering medical attention. To this day my nose is crooked. The inmate recovered, but I never saw him again. He ended up in the M-building because he couldn't live peaceably in the inmate population.

Although I deeply regretted the incident, other prisoners were impressed with my toughness. I was not tough; I was simply a part of the violence. There were many fights, and I didn't win them all.

Living with some of the most dangerous men on earth, I immediately learned that I needed a source of income. Money was power, and power was the key to survival. Cash was illegal, but inmates who had money in their account were issued a book of coupons to trade at the prison store for shaving items, candy, soft drinks, cigarettes, and the like. Model prisoners were allowed to go to "store call" once a week.

My money had run out long ago in the county jail, and there was no one to send more to me because I had no contact with my family. Some inmates had small businesses such as a leather works, but I had no money to get started. I couldn't borrow since I had no way to repay. (In prison, failure to pay a debt was an invitation to death.) Drugs were the big trade, but I didn't want to become involved. Stealing was out of the question. Hustling was my only option.

An unexpected break came with the clerk-typist job, which proved to be one of the most powerful inmate positions in the prison. Any prisoner who was too sick to work needed a lay-in slip from the doctor excusing him from his job until after he was examined. A form listing the inmate's name, number, and job was pinned to the bulletin board.

When the prisoners learned that I typed these forms and had the power to lay in anyone at will, one of the inmate leaders approached me.

"I've got a leather business, and I need some help tomorrow," he said. "How about laying in some workers for me? I'll give you four packs of cigarettes."

Other inmates offered similar proposals, and several asked me to lay in their homosexual lovers. I turned down every request. One day a friend came to me with a sad story of bad luck in a card game. To settle the debt he had paid all his money and had given away his shoes. For fifteen packs of cigarettes he could buy back the shoes. He wanted to borrow some cigarettes, but I had none to lend. I came up with a plan.

"Find me five men who will give you three packs each. In return, when I go to work tomorrow, I'll lay them in for the next day."

He arranged the deal and used the cigarettes to buy his shoes. In another game two days later, he lost them again! I refused to try the scheme a second time.

"I'll line up the people, you lay them in, and we'll split fifty-fifty," he begged. "You won't know the inmates, and they won't know you. If you get caught, you can swear that you never met them."

Having nothing, I was desperate, too. So we went into business. Although I was very careful, the hospital administrator soon found out and threatened to have me sent to the hole. I wasn't worried because both of us knew he couldn't replace me. I did his work, and he received the credit. He needed me, and I needed him. I asked him to sign a stack of slips so that I could lay in a man whenever I wanted. He agreed.

Periodically, physicians from Talmadge Memorial Hospital in Augusta, Georgia, held clinics on internal medicine, orthopedics, neurology, and other fields. I set up the X-rays, transcribed the tapes that contained instructions for an inmate's medical care, typed a note to the drug room stating the medication to be dispensed, and filled out the forms authorizing inmates to be transferred to Talmadge Memorial for surgery.

A number of inmates asked me to send them to the Augusta hospital so they could escape, and once I was offered $1,000 to do it. I refused the money, but compassion later persuaded me to help two men who had served many years in prison after being unjustly prosecuted. I believed in them and felt they would not be a danger to society. I could only get them out of the building; they had to overpower the guards, and they promised they would not harm them. The escape attempt failed, and I refused to help a second time.

The prison doctor and I were in his office one day when an inmate opened the door. He was obviously very disturbed.

"Doc, can I see you?" he asked.

"Come on in," the doctor said.

The inmate sat down and looked around suspiciously.

"What's on your mind?" the doctor began.

The inmate stared at me without answering.

"He's just my clerk," the doctor said. "Go ahead and say what's on your mind."

"They're after me," he said.

"Who's after you?"

"The people on television. They're after me."

"The people on television are after you?" the doctor repeated.

"Yeah, every time I look at television, they're looking at me. They're watching me. They're after me. And that ain't all. The warden stings me. He's got a button he pushes. It shocks me, and it hurts."

Suddenly he jumped out of the chair and screamed, "He's doing it again! Ow!" He bolted out the door and ran down the hall screaming. Guards finally overpowered him and carried him to the psychiatric ward.

I watched him and wondered, *Am I next? Will that be me one day?*

CHAPTER 6

HONOR AMONG THIEVES

Along with other inmates assigned to the hospital floor, I sometimes had to work around the clock assisting the doctors in emergencies. That's how I met Adams, one of the guards who worked the night shift. He was a kindly man in his sixties who never raised his voice or punished an inmate. He seemed very fatherly and often took me aside at night to talk. Only one person in the prison—an inmate doctor— knew that my mother was living. But I finally confided in this dear old man who seemed to think inmates were human.

"Please, Harold, let your mother know where you are," he urged. "She's worried about you. Why don't you write her and tell her you love her?"

I shook my head. "I can't," I said sharply. "I can't let her know how low I've sunk. She doesn't deserve that."

Adams sighed, and his eyes were full of compassion—a quality I rarely saw anymore. "Give it some thought, Harold," he urged again. "There's nothing harder on a parent than not knowing."

By this time I had been in prison for three-and-a-half years. My mom hadn't heard from me for more than seven years. For all she knew, I was dead. Although I often wished I would hear from my family and old friends, I couldn't face the possibility of rejection if they found out about me.

Adams continued to be kind to me. Although he frequently encouraged me to write my mother, he did not pressure me, and he never judged me for being in prison. Sometimes I thought about how much I had wanted that kind of understanding and acceptance from my father.

Then one night as we talked, Adams clutched at his left arm, gasping for breath. Suddenly he fell over, and several inmates jumped toward us to help. We moved Adams to the operating room, but there was no doctor on duty. One of the inmates started mouth-to-mouth resuscitation, but it was useless. Adams died.

For a few moments I stood there, and then I went to my cell. The years in jail and now prison had hardened me somewhat, and yet I felt deep grief over the death of someone I had considered to be a friend. I sat on my bunk and sobbed. Once I was back in control, I returned to the hospital.

When Adams' wife and daughter arrived at the prison hospital, they were not allowed to come to the floor where we were. One of the guards told us that the widow was very upset. As Adams' body was taken out, several inmates talked about him and the kindness he had shown. One said to me, "He was one of the finest men I've ever met."

"Do you really mean that?" I said.

"Man, I sure do!" he replied.

"Then let's write a letter to his wife." I sat at the typewriter and got a statement from each man, ending the letter with a note from all of us.

"This may not mean much to you, coming from inmates, but your husband was one of the finest men we have ever met. We really did care about him. Your loss is our loss." I asked a guard to deliver the letter.

The next day, Mrs. Adams came back to the prison and told the warden that she wanted to see the man who had written the letter. When a guard brought me in, she said, "So you're the one who wrote it."

Thinking she was angry, I hastily explained, "Yes, ma'am, but I wrote it for all the men."

I expected her to say, "You have nerve, a convict writing to me!" Instead, she hugged me and said, "Young man, I can't tell you what that letter has meant to me. I was married to a good man—one of the finest on earth. I'll never forget this."

She asked the warden if the men who had written the letter could attend her husband's funeral. Each one of us had at least one life sentence, and if we'd had a truckload of hacksaws, we couldn't have sawed our way out of prison. Yet this lady had requested that we be allowed to attend the funeral service in a little farming community several miles from the institution.

The warden didn't know what to do. Could he trust thirteen desperados? He brought us all together in a room on the hospital floor.

"Nothing like this has ever happened," he said. "I can't let you out because I know some of you will escape. But the whole family has requested that you come," he added, still undecided. "If I let you go, would you escape?"

I spoke. "No, sir, I wouldn't. I would never cause any disturbance for that family. The old man meant too much to me. As much as I want to escape, I won't." Each man gave his word.

"I'm going to do something I've never done before," the warden said. "I'm going to trust you. My job's on the line, but I'm going to let you go. I'll not allow the guards to wear guns inside that church. If you try to escape, it will be embarrassing."

It was about twenty miles from the prison to the church. We arrived early—dressed in our prison clothes. Unarmed guards marched us inside to a wing where we could sit together: thirteen desperados, able—yet unwilling—to run.

The church soon filled. It was a sad time for all of us. As soon as the service ended, we were taken through the back door to board the prison bus. The widow walked over to us, along with one of her sons. He said, "We feel honored that all of you would come. My dad spoke of you, and he didn't look down on you. Thank you for your behavior. This means a lot to my family."

During the trip back to the prison, we were all thinking the same thing. Our thoughts were put into words by an inmate who had spent twenty-one years in prison for killing a police officer.

"If anybody had told me that I could be in the woods like this and not run, I'd have said he was crazy. It breaks my heart to go back to that prison, knowing I'm going back to die. But I couldn't run. The old man meant too much to me."

All of us felt proud that day. We had been called animals, but we weren't. We not only proved that we could behave in a civilized manner, but also showed compassion, sort of repaying our friend for the love he had shown us.

Thirty minutes later, we were back in our cells. Though it was one of the saddest days of my life, I learned something about myself. I had cried when an old man died, and animals don't cry.

For some time I had wondered if I were, indeed, still human. Working on the hospital floor brought me into daily contact with the dying, many of whom were victims of dehumanizing cruelty. I measured stab wounds on corpses and took photographs of rape victims to be used as evidence against the offender. There was little I could do for these men, and most times, I despaired of trying. There was *one* thing I *could* do, though.

On Tuesdays the prison doctor treated inmates in the hole, and I assisted. Knowing that most of the men had been placed there unjustly and that they received only one meal of bread and water a day, I carried candy and smoking tobacco concealed under my shirt. I'd look at an inmate and nod my head as a signal for him to distract the guard. He'd fake a fight, then I'd toss the treats into the cell for the men to share. They'd look at me with desperate eyes—eyes that said "thank you."

But the doctor saw it all. "If the guards catch you, you'll be in here with them," he warned. I threatened to quit my job if he reported me.

Why would I want to risk going to the hole to help men I didn't even know—men who, under other circumstances, might want to rob or rape or murder me? At the time, even I probably didn't really understand. But many of the men thanked me later, and it gave me satisfaction to express compassion, though it be small. The ability to be compassionate in an inhuman situation was proof to myself that I had not yet become an animal. I was still a human being.

Nonetheless, prison existence proved daily that when men are treated like animals, they will do whatever is necessary to survive. Consequently, violence became a way of life. I never got used to it. Although I'd been a physical person and athletic, I realized brute strength was no match for psychopathic killers, and I was terrified. It was a rare thing for anyone to be prosecuted for murdering an inmate, and the penalty was usually an additional sentence to run concurrently with the existing one. That hardly served as a deterrent to murder.

Much of the violence in prison is drug related. One time, there were rumors that the black man in the bunk next to mine had ratted on a drug transaction, causing two inmates to get busted. One night while hallucinating on LSD, those two men held him down as a third man gouged his eyes out. It was one of the most horrible things I ever witnessed. In the morning the inmates who committed this heinous deed moaned in regret, "Why did we do it? He was our friend." Adding to the tragedy, the blinded man was later proven innocent.

Although inmates occasionally found a way to smuggle in narcotics, ninety percent of the drugs were brought in by the guards. A small risk netted a large gain of several thousand dollars. Whenever a guard got caught, he was asked to resign. Yet he'd be given a letter of recommendation. After all, the only witnesses were inmates.

The guards would deal with an inmate whom they felt they could trust, preferably a lifer who seemed a fairly decent guy. They approached me many times about being a contact person to sell drugs to other inmates. An inmate could obtain any drug he wanted, if he had money or cigarettes to trade. A marijuana joint the size of a big matchstick sold for two dollars and a "black beauty" for eight to twelve dollars.

Most of the men preferred drugs that could be injected, although those were more expensive. Many inmates who injected drugs later developed such serious infections from unclean needles that an arm or leg had to be amputated. Several developed hepatitis. Other drug users became blind, and some lost their hair. A young boy became a vegetable after sniffing paint thinner from a plastic bread sack. He died six months later, and his unclaimed body was buried in the prison graveyard.

But drugs were not the only catalyst for violence. Rage and hatred fed on the bigotry that men brought with them into prison, and racial tension was a constant companion. In order to survive, I quickly learned to never interfere when hostilities broke into physical violence. Many times I lay in my bunk and cried because I could do nothing to help the dying. And just as no one could depend upon me to rescue them, I never counted on anyone to stand by me. When my life was on the line, any inmate who chose to fight for me would end up fighting for his life, too.

It was every man for himself, and in the end I was alone. Knowing this helped me to survive. It's true that many inmates did help, but I never expected that. I knew they would stay with me only to a point. There would come a time when I'd have to draw the line and say, "He's not dependable." I didn't put myself into many situations in which I had to depend on them.

A Puerto Rican who shared my cell proved to be an exception. One day, several black inmates walked into our cell with weapons and started to jump me and another man. We were unarmed. The Puerto Rican—who was not respected by blacks or whites—pulled a knife out of his mattress and took a firm stand beside me.

"Me fight is for Big Harold!" he declared.

The attackers backed off and left. Puzzled as to why the Puerto Rican had defended me, I said, "I'll never forget this. There's nothing I won't do for you."

Smiling broadly, he said, "You my friend. You my friend."

In spite of my friendship with this Puerto Rican, I didn't overcome my racism. I particularly hated blacks. And that prejudice wasn't unique to me. Racial bigotry was widespread throughout the prison, and it often resulted in race riots. They usually ended within minutes without bloodshed. The inmates would drop their weapons, flee to their cells, and slam their doors. Sometimes, however, there was a bloodbath, as was the occasion one day in 1972 when several inmates were killed. A group of whites was attacked by black prisoners using homemade weapons they had buried on the athletic field. Hundreds were involved in the fight. Inmates smashed wooden benches and used the long splinters for stabbing. I ran for my life. Fear of being shot for trying to jump the fence no longer mattered in the face of a more horrible kind of death.

When the riot ended, the athletic field resembled a battleground, strewn with bleeding bodies. Helicopters were called in from the army base at Fort Stewart to transport the wounded to area hospitals. Miraculously, I escaped injury, but one of my buddies had been stabbed in the chest. Another friend helped me place him on a stretcher and carry him to an ambulance. We climbed in with him, and in all the confusion, no one noticed that two desperados had left the prison.

The other inmate was serving three life sentences. Knowing that we would die in prison, both of us wanted to run.

But at that moment we had a greater priority: helping to save the life of a friend.

When guards discovered that we had left the prison, an all-points bulletin was issued. As the ambulance arrived at Talmadge Memorial Hospital in Augusta, 110 miles away, armed guards surrounded us.

"Wait a minute," the ambulance driver said as we were being handcuffed. "Those men could have jumped out every time I had to stop at a traffic light. They could have taken me hostage, but they didn't. Don't treat them that way." They ignored him and shackled us like animals for the return trip.

My friend recovered, and knowing I valued his life more than my freedom made me feel good about myself. Again, I'd shown myself that I had compassion, even for a fellow inmate.

Many times I regretted that I didn't escape that day because it was the only chance I was to have for five years. But part of me felt glad that I hadn't run, for it taught me something very important. There *is* honor among thieves.

CHAPTER 7

GAMES CONVICTS PLAY

Prison life is unpredictable, and I never knew what was going to happen next. My job changed many times for various reasons. After working for a year as clerk-typist, I was busted following an incident with a guard. He ordered me to open a drawer that I had not been authorized to open, and when I refused, he called me a derogatory name. I took a swing at him, and he reported my behavior to the warden. Although the doctor pleaded my case, I lost the job, along with its power. My new assignment was in the laundry, where I worked alongside homosexuals.

I'd been kicked down many times in life, but my competitive spirit always brought me to the top again. Whenever my high school coaches penalized me, I worked my way back; whenever I was punished in prison, I did the same. A sense of humor helped me endure the worst of times.

Once, I asked an inmate, "How much time do you have?"

"Twenty years," he said.

"Great! Mail this letter on your way out!"

An inmate who worked as a cook for the guards had quite a drug problem. He really lived for drugs. I'd heard him say, "If they would give me all the drugs I wanted for two years, I would let them kill me. I'd sign a pact right now."

One Saturday during visitation hours he said, "Man, I'd give anything in the world for some drugs. You know Roger

pretty well. His girlfriend is visiting. See if she has any drugs.
I'll give you anything if you'll help me."

Roger had been in and out of prison all his life on petty
theft and burglary charges to support his drug habit. I told
him what the cook wanted and asked the girl if she had any
pills.

"Just birth control pills," she said.

"Give me one," I said. I walked away and motioned for
the cook.

"I made a score, but you have to take it quick! I don't
want to get in trouble."

He swallowed it, and half an hour later he staggered up
to me.

"That's the best drug I ever had in my life! It's dynamite!
I'll give you a carton of cigarettes if you'll get me one more."

"You really are high," I agreed. "And I'll tell you something else. You'll never get pregnant. That was a birth control
pill!" He chased me through the grounds for an hour.

One of the social trends that came and went while I was
in prison was streaking. Television kept us informed about
this fad, which was particularly popular on college campuses.
I bet an inmate a carton of cigarettes that he didn't have the
nerve to streak past the guard station, make a circle, and
run back to the dorm.

"I'll do anything for a carton of cigarettes," he said, stripping. He ran out of the dormitory, circled the station where
a dozen or so guards were on duty, and dashed back into
the dorm. Before he got there, I slammed the door, locking
him out. There he stood—stunned and buck-naked—threatening to kill me. The guard roughly escorted him (without
a stitch of clothes) to the hole for fourteen days of solitary
confinement. Everybody laughed, including the guards, but
as I thought about his humiliation, I felt ashamed. I determined to temper my practical jokes.

Tempering them was one thing, but limiting them to inmates was another. Nothing tickled me more than taking the
guards for a ride.

For three years I worked in the control office, the prison operations center. When one of the guards, Smith, started giving me a hard time, I threatened, "You'd better be nice to me or I'll have you assigned to tower six."

Tower six was the most undesirable assignment for a guard, frequently used as a disciplinary measure. By sheer coincidence, when Smith clocked in the next day, he was assigned to tower six. I had nothing to do with it, of course, but he didn't know. He sent a note by an inmate trusty.

"Please get me off tower six! I never thought I'd see the day that inmates would run the prison!"

I wrote back, "I'll think about it."

The next day Smith returned to regular duty. Again, I was not involved, but I saw no need to tell him. I had him where I wanted him.

"I really appreciate this," he said. "I'll throw a favor your way."

After that incident, Smith would do anything for me. When he caught me stealing chicken from the mess hall, instead of throwing me in the hole, he said, "Bring me a piece, too." After one of my buddies was busted, I persuaded Smith to plead with the guard to drop the charges.

Another guard told me he wanted Smith's job and planned to have him moved. So I warned my friend that his job was in danger.

"I won't ever forget this," he said. "You saved me."

Although my tactics with this guard may have been less than honorable, many inmates were helped as a result. His attitude toward them changed, and he stopped taking advantage of them and punishing them without cause. I didn't abuse the relationship; I used it in a positive way.

Another of my choice assignments was in a little hobby shop located at the edge of the prison. The shop carried hand-crafted leather items made by the inmates, and I sold these items to the public. The money was credited to their accounts, providing a few dollars to buy cigarettes, candy, and soft drinks. Although there was no money in it for me,

I gained a great deal of prestige because I was dealing with the outside world (though still in my prison clothes). Each day a guard drove me from my building to the shop.

"How'd you get a job like this?" asked an old guard who was uneducated and particularly surly whenever he was outsmarted by the inmates.

"Don't you know?" I dropped the bait.

"Know what?"

"Promise you won't tell anybody?"

"I promise."

"The warden is my brother."

He thought about that for a minute.

"But his name is Bradley and yours is Morris," he said.

"That's his maiden name," I explained.

"Oh, I see!" he said.

I laughed all day, knowing that he was telling the other guards, "You better be nice to Morris. He's the warden's brother. 'Bradley' is only the warden's maiden name."

The next morning he was livid. "You got a smart mouth, ain't you? I'll get you. You'll go to the hole!" he threatened. I knew I was safe. If he brought charges, he would have to tell what had happened!

Another guard walked over to the shop window one day.

"Hey, convict! I want the best wallet you've got," he said.

I reached for a hand-tooled wallet of quality leather—the nicest one in the shop—and handed it to him.

"You must think I just drove up here yesterday," he growled. "You think you can just sell me anything. I said I want the best you've got!"

It *was* the best, but I didn't try to convince him.

"I apologize, sir. I should have known the minute you walked up that you were different. You know your leather. I have just the wallet for you."

I picked up a wallet constructed of thin scrap leather. It had been stamped in a press without a hint of hand-tooling.

"That's more like it," he said. "How much is this one?"

At $1.25, the wallet was overpriced; by my figures the cost

of materials came to a mere sixty-seven cents. But we sold them for twelve dollars a dozen.

"For you, it'll be six dollars," I said. He whipped out the money. "I'll tell you what I'm gonna do," I went on. "Since it's you, and you know your leather, I'll give you a special deal if you'll take three dozen. It's close to Christmas, and you'll be the most popular daddy in the world if you buy these for your family. Three dozen for forty dollars."

"My goodness! I'll take 'em!" he said.

As he laid the money down, obviously delighted with his purchase, I said, "Let me show you a fine wallet." I reached for one that had been in the shop longer than I'd worked there. The inmate who had the job before me predicted that I'd never be able even to give it away. I'd tried several times without success.

"It's too bad that you can't own one of these," I said.

The curious old guard wanted to know more about the wallet.

"You can't buy it. It's not for sale," I hastened to add.

When an inmate tells a guard that he can't do something, it triggers his "I've-got-the-gun-and-I've-got-the-power" reaction.

"How come it ain't for sale?" he demanded.

"There will never be another one like it," I explained. (Really, there never *would* be another one like it!)

"How come?" He was determined to draw the truth out of me.

"This is imitation alligator," I said.

He gave me a puzzled look and hesitated a moment before asking, "What kind of gator is that?"

I realized he didn't know what imitation alligator was.

"The alligators were brought over from Australia," I began in a serious tone. "They would breed only with a south Georgia alligator. Don't ask me to explain that. I don't know why. But they wouldn't breed with another gator. Because those imitation gators are now extinct, this is it," I declared, holding up the wallet.

"I want it!" he insisted.

"Sir, you're an officer, and I can't deny you. I'll tell you what—you can have it for twenty-five dollars."

He counted out the money and picked up the one-of-a-kind wallet. I could almost hear him boasting to his buddies, "There'll never be another one of these. It's imitation alligator. The gators were brought over from Australia and bred right here in south Georgia." The humiliation would probably force the old man to resign his job.

I loved playing games like that, but I was not the only inmate with enthusiasm for outsmarting the guards. One of my cellmates, Andy, also enjoyed playing tricks. In spite of his tragic life story, he had quite a sense of humor. Andy had been placed in a detention center at the age of thirteen after stealing an automobile, but he fled the center by stealing one of the guard vehicles. For that offense he was sent to the county jail.

Tall and skinny, the boy suffered from diabetes. Smoking pot had also affected his health. He was double-jointed and so limber that I could stuff him into the small locker in our cell, making it appear to the guards that he had escaped.

I'd straighten Andy's bed and then stretch out on my bunk, pretending to be asleep when the guard came by to count.

"One," he'd say as I stifled a chuckle, knowing he would not be able to explain the discrepancy in his report. Shortly, I'd hear the guard and the captain approaching in a heated argument.

"You never could count!" the captain accused.

"I swear there ain't but one! I'll show you," the guard insisted.

I'd help Andy out of the locker in time for him to settle down on his bunk as though he'd been asleep all the while.

"There's two, you idiot!" the captain shouted.

"I'm telling you, there was just one!"

"You're through! I'm going to put you in tower six," the captain promised, his curses fading down the corridor as

Andy and I nearly died laughing. When the guard counted two hours later, we'd pull the prank again.

But prison is still prison, and sooner or later, all the laughter stops. It stopped for Andy after he was moved to another cell, where he was sexually assaulted by older convicts. Soon afterward, he hanged himself. Although I grieved for him, I was not surprised. The first violent act that I witnessed at Georgia State Penitentiary was the brutal rape of a young boy by an older man. It was the most humiliating thing I ever witnessed, and there was nothing I could do to stop it. When it was over I went to the toilet and vomited.

Although inmates were sentenced to the hole for being involved in homosexuality, the practice was widespread. Many older men "married" the young boys they had victimized. If a man lost a great deal of money in a poker game, he would sell his boy to settle the debt. During the night, the homosexuals and their lovers tied sheets around their bunks for privacy and called the rig a "covered wagon."

One either learns to accept homosexuality or he comes to hate it. Although most inmates initially despised the perversion, they had to accept it as a part of prison life. For eleven years, one inmate attacked every homosexual who approached him. Finally, under the influence of drugs, he performed a homosexual act. It was a sad turning point. He learned to accept homosexuality, and he pursued it as a lifestyle.

One of the other inmates had entered the prison with a life sentence. He was married to a beautiful woman who visited him every weekend. One day he told his faithful wife not to return and removed her name from his list of visitors. When she began to cry and question his reasons, he said he had found someone in prison whom he loved more. Eventually he divorced his wife for the homosexual lover.

I'm convinced the problems destroying our prisons—primarily drugs and homosexuality—could be corrected. I believe that eighty-five percent of the men in prisons throughout the country participate in homosexual behavior, and that the practice is also widespread in women's prisons. One female inmate in a state penitentiary estimated that at least seventy-five percent of the women were practicing lesbians.

I was disgusted and repulsed by those who practiced the homosexual lifestyle, but as a young boy, I had learned a valuable lesson from my father—one of the few things that I ever learned from him. He taught me that the greatest mark of any man is the ability to communicate on all levels. In prison, survival was very much a matter of understanding and communicating. I had the ability to communicate with young men and old, with tough men and weak, and I knew I had to learn to communicate with homosexuals if I wanted to survive. I did not have to adopt their lifestyle, but I did choose not to interfere with it.

Man needs purpose and meaning in life. After studying and analyzing fellow inmates, I reached the conclusion that those who survived—including myself—had established goals for living. They had a plan, and that plan gave hope. My plan was to stay one step ahead of the guards and the inmates, outsmarting them whenever possible. The challenge was to convince them to see things my way and yet be accepted by them. I would not live by their rules; I would not follow the convict code.

Then one day I chose to disregard my own survival code. I chose to intervene in a death plot, and that choice almost cost me my life.

CHAPTER 8

DEATH ROW

An inmate who was "anybody" received a name. It might be based on the crime he had committed, his job at the prison, his appearance, or his personality.

The most dangerous man in the Georgia State Penitentiary was known as Mad Dog. A former professional boxer with a tremendous physique, he had an extremely hot temper. Fortunately, he thought the world of me! We shared a cell and grew to be friends.

Someone reported seeing Mad Dog's girlfriend smuggle marijuana to him by hiding it in a prison Coke machine, so she was not allowed to visit him again. Mad Dog became hysterical and swore he'd kill the man who had ratted on him. He remembered that an inmate named Don had "looked at him" when his girlfriend hid the marijuana. He concluded it must have been Don, who happened to be another of my buddies.

A few days later, Mad Dog was sitting on his bunk when two of his friends came in. One sat on his bed, the other on mine, and they began talking about Don.

"I'm sure he did it," Mad Dog said. "Hey, isn't he your friend?"

"Yeah," I said.

"Do you think he did it?"

"I've never known him to do anything like that," I said.

"Well, we know he did it. He must die," Mad Dog decided. They plotted the murder for Saturday morning in the theater.

One of the men would send for Don, and when he arrived, the other man would kill him. Mad Dog would furnish the weapon.

I couldn't believe Don had ratted on Mad Dog, and I had to let him know he was in danger. Although he lived in another dormitory, I saw him at chowtime.

"Did you do it?" I asked.

"What are you talking about?" he asked. He knew nothing about the incident.

"They're going to kill you Saturday morning," I warned. "Please stay away from the theater."

Fearing for his life, Don told prison officers. They knew that if I'd said it, it must be true. Guards came to my dorm to shake down Mad Dog, looking for a weapon. It wasn't hard to figure out who had ratted about the murder plot, since I was the only other person who knew. Mad Dog refused to look at me.

Because the guards knew of my involvement, Mad Dog didn't dare kill me himself; instead, he put out a contract on me. When I heard about the contract, I didn't know what to do. I could "catch out"—that is, move to M-building with the other inmates who had received death threats. But it would be an isolated life, with meals served in the cell. I'd lived that way for more than two years at Fulton County Jail and for eight weeks at the penitentiary when I first arrived. I decided I'd rather be dead than to live in isolation again. Finally, I faced Mad Dog and his friends.

"Listen to me. You think I'm a snake? I'm not. I saved an innocent man's life. Don didn't rat about the drugs. I don't want any trouble, but I'm not running."

After three weeks went by without a calamity, I became a little cocky, thinking I was out of danger. As I stepped out of the shower one night, I felt an impulse to look up. Just in time I saw an inmate coming with a board. A split-second move to the side saved my life, but the board smashed the side of my head. I grabbed the man and choked him until guards pulled me away. Blood gushed from my head and from a cut on my arm. I thought I was bleeding to death. An inmate closed the head wound with thirty-nine stitches, and the next day I was in kangaroo court, on trial for inciting a riot in the dormitory.

The inmate who attacked me received fourteen days of solitary confinement. Afterward, he returned to his prison job. I was sentenced to the hole for fourteen days, and after that, to death row for as long as I remained at the institution. With two life sentences, that meant forever!

Death row was supposed to be reserved for those who had been sentenced to die. Being placed there illegally, I could have brought charges, if I had known my rights.

The warden might have prevented this unjust discipline, but he didn't know about it. The deputy warden knew—and didn't care. He walked by as I was being taken to death row with my hands cuffed behind my back.

"They've just sentenced me to death row forever!" I cried.

The hatred of many years rose in his voice as he said with a satisfied laugh, "Nothing lasts forever."

There is no hope among condemned men. On death row the desperate wait to die. Some eighty men were there when I arrived.

I looked around at my new accommodations: another eight-by-ten foot cell with a bunk, a small sink offering only cold water, and a commode permanently cemented to the wall to resist the strength of the insane, who would attempt to rip the fixtures from their mountings. There wasn't enough room to exercise, and it appeared the cell hadn't been swept in six months. The door was padlocked. I would be allowed to leave the cell only once a week to shower. I had one shirt and one pair of pants; underwear, socks, and belts were not allowed, to reduce the possibility of death by hanging.

Meals—usually cold—came on a tray pushed under the door three times a day. A television mounted on the wall outside the cell was controlled by the guards. It did not help to pass the hours, because I found it difficult to view a program through the bars. There was constant noise, and the pressures, I can't begin to describe.

"Hey, next door," someone called through the metal partition that separated our cells.

"Yeah?" I answered.

"If I get out of this cell, I'm going to kill you!"

A man I'd never even seen wanted to kill me! My own kind didn't want to live with me! The first day on death row, I knew I was through.

Later I learned that my violent neighbor had been convicted of murder. After being sentenced to prison, he had killed a guard and an inmate. He swore he'd kill again, and I was to be his next victim. Thank God, we were never out of our cells at the same time.

The man in the cell to my right had murdered thirteen people. Alone in my filthy cell, sandwiched between two killers, I entered the darkest days of my life.

Lying in bed, I looked at the metal wall and noticed a word that had been crudely scratched there. "Help." Month after month I stared at it. I could almost see the man who had written the message. In my imagination I watched his face as he heard someone call, "All right, number seven, you're next. Time to go to the electric chair." Hopeless, he scratched on the wall a last plea for help and walked out the door to his death. The reality of it almost drove me crazy.

What does it take to be broken? I'd survived prison violence with numerous wounds, culminating in thirty-nine stitches in the head. I'd survived prison punishment and the continual taunting of guards. I'd survived the loneliness—five years without receiving a letter or a visitor because I was too ashamed to let my family know where I was. But the absolute hopelessness is what finally broke me. After six months on death row, I simply gave up.

Convinced that I would never get out of prison, or off of death row, I decided to take my life. Having worked on the hospital floor, I was familiar with the solution used to test for diabetes. Taken internally, it would be fatal. I asked the inmate who brought my meals to steal a small quantity of the solution for me. I promised to give him everything I owned. That didn't consist of much—my shoes and a little money in my account. He said he would try.

I didn't want to die. But I had evaluated my life, and I saw no reason to continue. Although I was physically strong enough to survive, I didn't want the kind of existence I'd known for five years. I wrote a letter to my mother.

"I love you, and I'm sorry I've disgraced you. I don't want to die, but I can't live under such horrid conditions any longer. You have been a great mother. Don't think that you have failed me. I have failed you. You're the best thing that ever happened to me. Please forgive me. I'm sorry."

Through a guard I sent word to one of my friends, an inmate I could trust. Stuart was a physician who had been convicted of sex and drug offenses. His trial was widely publicized, and many of the inmates at Fulton County Jail plotted to kill him. That made him the underdog—someone I automatically wanted to defend. When he arrived at Georgia State Penitentiary, we came to know each other well. He was one of the few people I told that my mother was still living.

Stuart was the kind of person I could talk to, and I wanted him to know about my plans for suicide. I also had a favor to ask of him. Because he was a physician, he was permitted to roam the prison, and he came as soon as he got my message.

When he came to my cell, I told him I had decided to take my life and asked him to see that my mother received the letter after my death.

"Please don't do it!" he pleaded. "If you'll wait, I'll go to the warden. You shouldn't be here. You're innocent. I'll do all that I can to get you out of here. Please give me a chance!" His eyes flooded with tears when I shook my head. It was hopeless, I told him.

When the inmate who delivered my meals came, he said

he had not been able to obtain the poison I wanted. How absurd! A man condemned to death row—and unable to die! I cried all night.

The next morning I sat in silence. I was completely broken. For as long as I could remember, I had steadfastly refused to believe in God. At the same time, I shook my fist in the air and *dared* Him to exist. Once, on the prison baseball field, I had screamed to the thundering skies that rained out our game, "I don't believe in You, God! If You are real, strike me dead!" There was no God. If He were real, how could He have allowed the things that had happened in my life?

Not only did I rant at a God I didn't believe in, I had also persecuted those who claimed a relationship with Him. Once, when a man came to my cell to tell me about Jesus Christ, I threw filthy water from the commode into his face.

Now I sat on death row, without hope, unable to live and unable to die. For the first time in my life I knelt and prayed.

"God, if You are real, take my life or free me! I can't stand this place anymore."

Two weeks later I was moved to the "trusty" building— the best place an inmate could hope to be within the prison. At that time it never occurred to me to give God the credit, and I soon forgot all about my prayer of desperation to Him.

Lifers rarely achieve "trusty" status. But after being informed by Stuart that I had been illegally sentenced to death row, the warden took it upon himself to elevate me to warden's trusty. Because of the injustice that had been done, he risked his job to make amends. I gave him my word that I would not escape, but I lied.

For five years I'd worked to get myself into a position to escape. Moving to the trusty building was the opportunity I'd been waiting for. The 450 or so inmates who lived in the facility at the edge of the prison property were considered trustworthy and therefore were given special privileges. The cell doors were locked only at night, giving us much more freedom than other inmates. On weekends we were allowed in the prison yard anytime before 6 P.M., though we still were counted every two hours.

After moving to the trusty building, I persuaded the warden to provide educational opportunities to the men in my building, since many of them could neither read nor write. Having an educational background, I was one of several inmates chosen to assist the teachers who came to the prison. I had studied Spanish in college, and since entering prison, I had completed a correspondence course in Spanish, mastering 1,500 vocabulary words. Because of this, I gave Spanish lessons to one of the teachers, a guard, and another inmate.

My motive was to brush up on my Spanish in preparation for my escape. Long ago I had accepted the fact that I would never be released from prison through legal channels. Escape was my only hope. My plan was to settle in a Latin American country and work on an oil rig.

I had become involved in sports about six months after arriving at the prison, but six months on death row had made me flabby. I started jogging to build my physical endurance, and then I persuaded the warden to let me organize a prison team.

One day toward the end of baseball season, I noticed a little boy who was sitting on a bench watching our game. I started toward him, but a guard stopped me. Because of some recent riots, security was tight. The next time he came to a game, the guard let me sit on the bench and talk to him. He was wearing a T-shirt that said "Jesus First!"

He told me his name was Cliff Miller, and he was twelve years old. His father was a state trooper, and his mother worked as a nurse at the prison. They lived on the prison reservation, he said, pointing to the white house where he was born. I had seen the house from my cell.

"You know I'm a convict, don't you?" I asked.

"I'm not afraid of you," he responded.

The little boy attended all our games that season, and we became great friends. He was curious about my life and asked many questions. The trusty building was directly in front of his house, and he came to the prison fence to see me almost every day. He always wore a T-shirt with a slogan, such as, "I'm OK, Jesus don't sponsor no losers!" Another shirt showed a man with flexed muscles and said, "I can do all things through Christ who strengthens me." I laughed at his shirts but not at the seriousness with which he shared his faith. Many times that little boy told me I needed Jesus in my life.

Cliff always had a basketball in his hands. His goal was to be the greatest basketball player in the whole world, and he was obviously a gifted athlete. We tossed the ball back and forth across the fence. Being a former all-state basketball player, I suggested leg exercises to build his strength and gave him pointers to improve his dribbling. I watched as he practiced up and down the road and around the guard tower, switching from his left hand to his right and dribbling between his legs.

We developed a strong friendship in spite of the wire barrier. While I instructed him about sports, he taught me about Jesus. Young Cliff was my only contact with the outside world, until one morning when a guard came to my cell and announced, "You have a visitor."

"I'm not going," I said, thinking it was an inmate from another building, possibly an attorney with legal papers, or even a counselor with news that my job was being changed. Those were the only visits I'd had during almost five years in prison. Not one person from the outside had come. I had not sent or received a letter, and there had been no phone calls.

"If you don't go, I'll put you in the hole," the guard threatened. I wasn't stupid. I went to see the visitor.

When I walked into the prison lobby, there stood my brother Carl. No woman could ever look more beautiful to me than he did that day. We hugged each other and instantly re-experienced the love that God wants us to have for each other.

"How could you do it?" he said. "How could you not let us know? We love you!"

I burst into tears as Carl told me that my mother loved me, and then he explained how he had found me. A neighbor in Georgetown, South Carolina, was looking through some old magazines at the beauty parlor when she came across a five-year-old copy of *True Detective*. There was my picture, along with an account of the crime I supposedly had committed.

"We found him!" she cried as she carried the news to Carl. He then traced me to Georgia State Penitentiary.

"Carl," I said finally, "Carl, I didn't kill that man."

"I know, Harold," he said.

I can't describe what it meant to learn that my family loved me and wanted to stand with me. I was no longer alone! Knowing that gave me hope.

Carl spent the day with me, and when he left, sadness engulfed me. That night I lay on my bunk reflecting on the events that had led me to such a place. Clearly, it all began in high school by drinking alcohol and running with the wrong crowd. Drugs came later, and the wrong crowd became desperados whose false testimony sealed my conviction. One who crawls with animals catches fleas. So it was in my life.

Through that long night of relived memories, I came to understand how pride had wrecked my life, even as it had destroyed Adam and Eve and multitudes since. A proud man looks down on people and things; he cannot see what is above—the God of Heaven. Pride kept me from calling my precious mother during the loneliest years of my life, adding to the unspeakable pain I was already facing.

But now, I had hope again—and a sense of anticipation. A few days later, I was allowed to make a five-minute phone call to my mother. It had been years since I'd heard her voice, and I waited nervously for the call to go through.

"Momma, I love you!" I cried. "Please forgive me!"

"I love you, son, and I'm proud of you," she said.

Proud of me? How could she be, I wondered. I could hardly wait for the next visitors day. From my cell on the second floor, I could see the visitors parking lot. I watched my family bring that dear gray-haired lady, walking with her head held high.

Any visitor is subject to search, even the stripping of all clothing if officials deem it necessary. I couldn't bear the thought of subjecting my precious mother to such humiliation. Why must one of the finest ladies on the face of the earth suffer when she was guilty of nothing except bringing me into the world? It broke my heart to realize how I'd hurt her.

When I asked her again to forgive me, she looked me straight in the eye and insisted, "Harold, I couldn't be more proud of anyone than I am of you. I thank God for your life."

Her words brought healing to my wounded soul as I began to understand that she saw worth and value in *me,* even if my behavior was questionable.

When I told my family of my plans to escape, they begged me to give them a chance to obtain my freedom through legal means. So I set aside my plans and settled down for what was to be a very long wait.

CHAPTER 9

LIBERTY TO
THE CAPTIVES

On the day of Carl's first visit, he asked me if I remembered Clebe McClary. Of course I remembered Clebe, a gifted athlete at Winyah High. We had played on the same football and basketball teams. He was a year younger than I, and after I graduated, he wore my football jersey.

My brother said that Clebe had been seriously wounded in Vietnam.

"He's preaching the gospel now, and he wants to visit you," Carl said. The last person I wanted to see was someone who preached the gospel. I didn't encourage the visit.

A few weeks later four of my old high-school buddies came to see me. They also mentioned that Clebe wanted to visit.

On the morning of February 18, 1974, a guard came to my cell saying that I had a visitor. When I walked into the prison lobby, I didn't recognize the man in the Marine uniform standing with his back turned to me. As he turned, I noticed a patch where his left eye should have been, and a mechanical hook had replaced his left arm. With his twisted right arm he held a Bible.

Could this war-mangled man be the former all-state athlete Clebe McClary? Two-thirds of his face had been blown away by grenades, but thirty operations had rebuilt his face and body. As he walked toward me a tear trickled down his right cheek. He was crying for me!

"I brought this to you," he said, clamping his hook around the Bible. I'd never owned a Bible. If the warden had said, "Quote John 3:16 and I'll set you free," I couldn't have done it.

"Let's pray," Clebe said. I couldn't let the warden and inmates see me pray! So I didn't close my eyes when he knelt.

"How are you fixed with the Lord?" he asked.

"There isn't much of a chapel program here," I mumbled. I was ashamed to tell him I didn't even believe in God. He told me that he loved me and that Jesus died for me. No one had ever told me that. He asked about the Atlanta crime and about prison life.

Clebe wanted me to meet his wife, Deanna, who had been waiting in the car. She was allowed to come to the door for just a few minutes. Deanna handed me a cassette of Clebe's testimony and a note listing several Bible verses that she asked me to read.

"Clebe and I love you, Harold," she said. "But more importantly, God loves you, and He's going to help you."

After they left I went to my cell on the top floor of the prison and watched them cross the parking lot. Clebe knelt beside the car, and I knew he was praying for me. I began to cry. Turning to the inmate who shared my cell, I said, "He loves me . . . he loves me!"

To think that I had felt sorry for myself while Clebe, in his pitiable condition, was showing concern for me—a convict who had never been sick a day! I was overwhelmed with sadness.

Locked in my cell that night, for the first time in my life I opened the Bible and started to read the verses Deanna had listed. There were more Johns than I'd known in my entire life! Finally I found 1 John 1:9: "If we confess our sins, He is faithful and just to forgive us our sins and to cleanse us from all unrighteousness." Romans 6:23 said, "For the wages of sin is death, but the gift of God is eternal life in Christ Jesus our Lord."

I read 1 Peter 2:24: "Who Himself bore our sins in His own body on the tree, that we, having died to sins, might live for righteousness—by whose stripes you were healed." Revelation 3:20 stated, "Behold, I stand at the door and knock. If anyone hears My voice and opens the door, I will come in to him and dine with him, and he with Me."

Deanna had also noted the first three chapters of Philippians. I didn't understand what they meant, but I read them again and again.

On the cassette tape, Clebe described the enemy attack in Vietnam that brought him face to face with death and the years of hospitalization and rehabilitation. He said the direction of his life was changed at a crusade where he heard Bobby Richardson, former all-star second baseman of the New York Yankees, share his faith in Christ, followed by a message by Billy Zeoli of Gospel Films. After that, both Clebe and his wife had committed their lives to Jesus.

Suddenly, the dam that held years of hatred and bitterness within me burst in a flood of tears. For hours I cried and read the Scriptures until I could no longer stand the strain. About 3 A.M. I fell to my knees in that filthy, roach-infested cell and cried out to Jesus, admitting my sin and begging His forgiveness. God heard the cry of my heart and cleansed my sin, filling me with joy and peace such as I have never known. The words of Psalm 102:19-21 became a reality:

> For He looked down from the height of His sanctuary;
> From Heaven the Lord viewed the earth,
> To hear the groaning of the prisoner,
> To loose those appointed to death,
> To declare the name of the Lord in Zion,
> And His praise in Jerusalem.

On February 19, 1974, a lowly sinner met the mighty Savior! The commitment I made that night was a body, soul, mind, and heart commitment to my Lord God.

A calm settled over my storm-ravaged flesh, and I marveled that my cellmate could sleep so soundly. When morning came and we reported for work, I heard my cellmate say to the lieutenant, "You'd better watch what you say around old Harold. He's now a Christian."

"What did you say?" I was taken by surprise.

"I said old Harold is now a Christian."

A Christian! A follower of Christ!

My reply was, "You just paid me the highest compliment I could ever receive. Thank you!"

Later in the day I penned a very special letter.

Dear Momma,
   I know you've prayed for me for thirty-five years. Last night I gave my heart to Jesus Christ. I wanted to let you know.

Love,
Harold

She was thrilled to hear that her baby boy had trusted Christ. "Son," she wrote, "I've prayed for you every day of your life. I'm so proud of you. Be a good boy, and let Jesus direct your life. My prayer is that before I die, I will see you become a free man and stand in my church to give your testimony."

The day that I gave my life to Christ, I joined a Bible study which had been organized by several inmates. The leader was a crippled boy named Ernie. I remembered when he trusted Christ. The guards declared him insane and carried him to the psychiatrist. The doctor made a surprising diagnosis: "That man is a Christian, and you need 400 more just like him."

Several inmates were in the room when I arrived for the Bible study. Ernie said, "Harold, I don't want any trouble."

For the first time I realized how I had behaved in front of those men. I had refused to live in the same dormitory with Christians because I couldn't trust them. I'd made it clear that I hated Christians and the make-believe God they served.

"Ernie, I didn't come to cause trouble," I said. "I gave my heart to Christ last night, and I want to join your Bible study. I have a tape I'd like for you to hear." After listening to Clebe's story, several inmates trusted Christ.

Having persecuted Christians, I didn't expect to escape persecution myself. Many times I was ridiculed for professing faith in Christ. Inmates called me a phony while guards labeled me a Jesus freak. I longed for some good-natured companionship.

One day as I crossed the grounds, I noticed my young friend Cliff dribbling his basketball up and down the road near the fence. When I shouted his name, he waved. As I wandered over to the fence, he tossed me the ball.

"What are you doing with a Bible?" he asked, pointing to my hand.

"I've become a Christian, and I'm going to Bible study," I explained.

He grinned and suggested we share some Scriptures. Of course, he knew ten times as many verses as I did.

"You're stupid," he teased.

"Come around to this side of the fence and say that again," I kidded back.

"Open the gate!" he told the guard.

The guards knew him, and at times he was allowed inside. When Clebe McClary led a crusade at the prison that summer, Cliff was in the front row.

The friendship of that little boy helped to make bleak days bearable. I was not prepared for the sad news that he brought in late 1974. His family had purchased a house in town and planned to move very soon.

"I've brought you something," he said, handing the gift through the fence. It was a wooden cross he had made using two small branches. He had shellacked them and added a string so I could hang the cross in my cell.

Growing in Christ was a slow process, and many times I

wondered if I'd ever be as mature in Christ as Cliff was! Sometimes I reverted to bad habits. I even smoked marijuana a few times. But as I studied God's Word, I learned to depend on the power of Christ in my life to overcome temptation.

On the basketball court one day, an inmate spit in my face and cursed my mother's name. Fury raged within me, but I knew I could not fight. I wept instead. It was the first time in my life that I had backed down from a challenge. Another inmate followed me to my cell, saying, "You're a coward! I never thought I'd see the day. You're through!"

"You don't understand," I said. "I'm not a coward. I've just become a man. Instead of fighting and hurting people, I want to help them." During the years that followed, many inmates came to me for help. I had taken a stand for right, and God honored that.

It's not easy living a Christian life behind prison bars. The noise is unbearable, and privacy nonexistent. I didn't know how to pray, but whenever I felt confused, I went to the shower and talked with God. It became a daily habit—seeking power in the shower! In the only privacy I could find, I emptied my heart to the Father. Others heard about my quiet place and soon joined me; together we learned about prayer.

Clebe sent several tapes, which I played for the men. On Sundays we met in the little prison chapel and sang hymns. After playing a tape I gave an invitation, and many came to know Christ. It was as close as we could come to a church service.

I persuaded the warden to bring Clebe back to the institution for a crusade on July 8. Murderers, robbers, rapists, and other violent criminals—120 of them—filled the little chapel. After Clebe spoke, sixty-six men bowed on their knees and gave their hearts to Christ.

Getting into God's Word was the key to growing in the Lord. Soon after trusting Christ, I gave a devotional for several men, starting in the book of Genesis. This grew into a Bible study, and in a little while I'd read all the way through the Scriptures. I read the Gospel of John over and over, finding myself especially drawn to chapters 3 and 11. Clebe also gave me Bible studies to share with the inmates. Even in prison, men were becoming disciples!

Several Christian laymen in the community received permission from prison officials to begin a discipleship program called Lay Institute for Evangelism, developed by Campus Crusade for Christ, International. They explained the program to a group of inmates and asked us to pray that a large number would take advantage of the study, which would begin on Thursday night, just fifty-four hours away.

"Why don't we begin a prayer chain?" I suggested. "How many are willing to pray around the clock?" Twenty-four inmates wanted to participate. Every man would pray at a designated hour during each of the two days, and several would take an extra hour the third day so that the chain remained unbroken.

The next day guards stopped by the office where I worked and expressed astonishment that when they counted at 3 and 5 A.M., they had found inmates on their knees. Some men spent the hour in the chapel reading the Bible and praying. Most of the inmates had never even been to church, but for fifty-four hours they were on the cement floor before God, learning the power of prayer.

When the study began on Thursday night, exactly fifty-four inmates enrolled—one per hour of prayer! Only thirty-one of us completed the study, but from the experience we learned of the magnificent power available to those who pray.

Several months after trusting Christ, I received a call from someone claiming to be my attorney. When I answered the phone it was Jack, one of the men who had testified against me.

"I think about you every day, Harold, and I'm sorry for what happened. I'll do anything in the world to help you," he said. He had married a rich girl and wanted to bring her to the prison to meet me. He said if I'd get an attorney, he'd make a statement that he had lied about my being involved in the crime.

"Do you really mean that?" I asked. He insisted that he did.

"My life is at stake!" I told him. He said he would come to the prison next Wednesday. I was overwhelmed that Jack would actually help me.

"Thank you! I'll never forget this! Man, I love you!"

I called my family, and they arranged with an attorney to meet with Jack. Wednesday came, but Jack never showed. It was a tremendous disappointment, having my hope built up only to be let down again.

As a volcano of anger and bitterness boiled up within me, I began to have another reason for wanting Jack to come— so that I could kill him! My cellmate vowed that if I didn't, he would. But I never heard from Jack again.

I knew from my Bible studies that there is no room in a Christian's life for hatred, and yet I continued to struggle with powerful feelings. Some of my hatred was directed against Jack and Danny, and much of it was ventilated in the form of racial prejudice.

One day the warden sent for me. By order of the federal government, he explained, every cell had to be integrated by the next day.

"You have until 4 P.M. today to have a black in your cell. I'm going to let you pick him."

Facing the possibility of spending the rest of my life in a cell with a black man, I approached Big Willie. He was the greatest natural athlete I'd ever seen, and he appeared to have a lot of class.

"Do you wash?" I asked.

"What are you talking about?" he demanded.

"Every white guy has to have a black in his cell," I explained. "I want one who will wash. I'll share everything I have with you, but you can't steal. You can't bring anybody in to mess with my things, and I'll protect yours."

"I wash every day," he said and promptly moved in.

Willie was a real classy guy, but living with a black man was a difficult adjustment for me. Whenever the door was open, we took advantage of the opportunity to get away from each other.

One day as we sat on our bunks just inches from each other, he said, "You don't like me, do you?"

"I hate you," I said. "And you don't like me."

"I hate your guts," he admitted. Then he probed, "Why do you hate me?"

I thought I could give fifty reasons for hating blacks, but for the first time I didn't have an answer.

"Because you're black," I finally said.

"My mother washed clothes for whites, and they treated her like dirt," he sneered. "I'm as good as you are." When he finished speaking, I was crying.

"I've been wrong," I said. "For a lifetime I've been taught to hate. Forgive me. I'll do anything to make it right with you." It didn't happen overnight, but eventually I learned to like him as I learned about him. At age eighteen he had been offered a contract with the Cincinnati Reds. He chose drugs instead, and came to prison with an eighteen-year sentence after robbing a finance company.

I grew to love Willie, and even arranged for him to work with me in the athletic department. Our relationship set precedents at the prison by fostering unity and reducing racial strife. The inmates called us "Salt and Pepper." Blacks gained respect for me and gave me a complimentary name—Super Honky.

I learned a great deal from Big Willie. An especially memorable lesson concerned loyalty. One night a gang of Black Muslims armed with weapons attacked a group of whites in which I happened to be included. When Willie tried to defend us, he got stabbed seven times. After he was carried to the hospital, I mopped up his blood, realizing that it was red like mine. I cried, knowing that he had risked his life for me. There was upheaval in my heart as I understood that Jesus' death 2,000 years ago was for the black man as well as the white man. The color of one's skin doesn't matter to our Father, only the purity of one's heart.

I fell to my knees and prayed that God would spare my friend's life. When Willie returned to the prison three months later, I knew the Father's hand was on him.

Every day Big Willie watched me read my Bible, and although he said he wasn't interested in spiritual things, I shared with him about my faith. One afternoon Clebe McClary came to speak at chapel, and I persuaded Willie to go with me.

He was captivated by this war-scarred Marine who invited inmates to surrender to Christ. When it was time to be locked up again, I was given a few minutes to visit with Clebe. I asked that Willie be allowed to stay. As Clebe put his arm around him and began to share, Willie knelt to receive Christ. He began reading the Bible every day, and the change in him was amazing.

When Christmas came, both of us felt sadness about being locked up, separated from our families. Late Christmas Eve, Willie shared the doubts he had gathered in his heart.

"We've been here all this time. We need to be with our families. We're Christians. I don't understand how God could allow this to happen."

"Big Willie, I know your thoughts," I said. "This is my ninth Christmas in prison. I'm depressed too. But I want to share something with you. The Apostle Paul was in a dungeon with his ankles in stocks. He couldn't walk around as you and I can in this cell. He didn't even have a commode. We have much for which to be thankful. We have each other, and people to love us. Your mother comes every weekend. We don't have anything materially, but we have the greatest possession on the face of the earth—Jesus Christ. And one day we're going to be joint heirs with Him!" I showed him Galatians 4:7: "Therefore you are no longer a servant but a son, and if a son, then an heir of God through Christ."

"Let me see that!" he said, reaching for the Bible. He

read the verse again and again. When he looked up he was smiling. "We are lucky, aren't we?" he said.

Like the Apostle Paul, we prayed and praised God with our voices while tears washed our faces. It was a very special time as the depression gave way to joy.

CHAPTER 10

NEW CREATURE

The promise of 2 Corinthians 5:17 is that a person in Christ becomes a new creature. That included convict 62345. Old habits and attitudes were replaced as the Spirit of God worked in my life. The vengeance that I had nourished for five years and the rebellious spirit that had been a driving force in my life relaxed their grip when Christ took control. Little by little He replaced my hatred with His love.

Sometimes I lay in the prison yard looking at the sky and relishing the joy and peace that I'd found in Christ. The bars and fences were still there, as were the guards with their high-powered rifles. But I had an inner strength I'd never known—the very presence of Christ!

Many times I prayed for my freedom and promised God that I'd serve Him with my life if I got out of prison. God knew that if I wouldn't serve Him in prison, I wouldn't serve Him in the free world. Finally I could say the words He had been waiting to hear: "Father, You know I want to be free. But if it's Your will that I stay in prison, I accept that. I'll serve You here with my life."

The result of that relinquishment was an improved relationship, not only with inmates but also with the warden and guards. Many times I talked with the warden about inmate rights. The counselors were holding our mail for days, and the inmates were planning to riot in protest. I pointed out to the warden that harmony was more desirable than rioting, and since mail brought harmony, it needed to be delivered on time.

I also suggested that he set up a special time once a week to listen to inmate concerns. Some of their requests were ridiculous, but they could accept a denial knowing he was willing to listen.

One of my suggestions that he carried out was to expand the athletic program. I helped put together a softball team that competed against other prisons and several junior colleges. We were the top prison team in the south.

I also persuaded the warden to let us organize a prison team to compete against the free-world team in Metter, Georgia, a small town thirty-four miles from the prison. Several guards were involved in a community league there, and I thought it would be good public relations, showing citizens that inmates are not animals. The warden liked the idea.

"But if a man runs, you'll never play again," he warned.

He allowed me to choose the players because he knew I wouldn't select someone who couldn't be trusted outside the prison gate. Several of the best players were eliminated because I knew that given a chance, they would run. Most of the inmates on the team had a life sentence. Though undisciplined, they were great athletes.

Nonetheless, the uncertainty of prison life affected athletics. Sometimes an athlete was killed in a fight or busted for drugs. Within a day I might have an entirely new team. During periods of violence the sports program would be canceled; at one time, the entire prison was locked down for a year.

Even so, the prison team was the obvious favorite of the townspeople. Competing against thirteen teams sponsored by local merchants, we won the league championship and captured every trophy offered. We won the state championship for three out of five years. A picture of the team still hangs in the prison—fourteen black inmates and me.

Athletics boosted inmate morale while improving the prison's image. After the softball team proved successful, the warden gave me permission to organize a basketball team to compete against others in Metter. When we won the league championship, the newspaper carried a picture of the team and the warden, who was holding the trophy.

Eventually, I was chosen to head the athletic department. The position involved organizing intramural teams, coaching the boxing teams, scheduling sports events, preparing the athletic fields, and issuing equipment. I also ran errands for the warden and handled special projects, such as marking the rifle range with lime for the guard's target practice. The job proved to be rewarding, and it gave me opportunities to do things I might not have had otherwise. It showed I could be trusted.

In 1973, normal prison routine was interrupted when actor Burt Reynolds and producer Al Ruddy paid a visit to Georgia State Penitentiary to determine whether the site would be suitable for filming a motion picture. They began work on September 15 for *The Longest Yard,* starring Reynolds. I was one of several inmates who were given roles in the football and swamp scenes. A catering service brought our meals to the filming sites.

My contract with Paramount studios offered $5 a day and an additional $50 every time I made contact in a football scene. One of the professional actors said jokingly to Burt, "Morris has a bigger part than I have!"

Prison officials wanted the inmates to stay away from the actors, but Burt often came to sit with us.

"Is it all right if I talk to you?" he said.

"Yes, sir," I replied.

"What are you in for?"

"Armed robbery and murder."

"You don't look like a murderer," he said.

"What does one look like?" I asked.

He wanted to know about my family and seemed genuinely interested in my life. We talked a great deal during the coming weeks.

One day a member of the camera crew started charging

inmates $2 each to have souvenir photographs taken with Burt. I had no money, and neither did several other inmates.

"Take all the pictures they want," Burt told the photographer. "I'll pay for them."

An old-timer who had been in prison for many years asked Burt, "Where do you live?" He said he had a home in Florida and one in California. The inmate asked for his address.

"Why do you want my address?" Burt wondered.

"I'm a professional thief, and all my life I've been stealing from people who ain't got nothing," he said without cracking a smile. "When I get out next week, I want to steal from somebody who's got something!"

Burt said, "He means that, doesn't he?"

When filming was completed on December 15, the movie crew gathered up their equipment and started to leave the prison.

"Do you think you'll ever get out?" Burt asked.

I said, "No."

"I wish you would. I'd give you a job tomorrow. Is there anything I can do for you?"

"Yes, I'd like to have some pictures for my nieces and nephews," I said. He took an hour to autograph fourteen photos, personalizing each with the name of the recipient and adding, "It was great being with your Uncle Harold."

I told him I'd like to have some good reading material. From that time on, I received a best-seller every month from the Book of the Month Club, compliments of Burt Reynolds.

The premiere of *The Longest Yard* took place at the prison in April, 1974. After viewing the motion picture, I was told the warden wanted to see me. *At 10 P.M.? Nobody ever went to his office at that hour.* When I walked in, I found the room jammed with members of the news media.

"Mr. Morris, I guess being in a movie with Burt Reynolds is the greatest thrill of your life, isn't it?" a reporter asked.

I said, "Ma'am, on February 19th of this year, I gave my heart to Jesus. That's the biggest thrill of my life."

I couldn't believe what I read in the paper later: "Harold Morris, a baby-faced gent—five down on a double-life sentence—said that being in a movie with Burt Reynolds was the biggest thrill of his life."

One day not long afterward, the warden sent for me. He explained that the people in the community had approached him about sending an inmate to speak in area high schools, informing young people about alcohol, drugs, and prison life. Of the 3,200 men at Georgia State Penitentiary, I had been chosen.

"There's no way I'll speak in public wearing these prison clothes with a number stamped on my back," I objected.

"We'll give you anything you want to eat," the warden bribed. The offer was too good to pass up.

"I'm your man!" I agreed.

The next morning a guard drove me to Ware County High School in Waycross, Georgia. Seeing the gymnasium packed with teenagers frightened me so much that I honestly thought about trying to escape. A hush fell on the students as I explained how alcohol and drugs had played a part in my going to prison.

I went on to say that one of the saddest experiences of prison is seeing wasted potential. Doctors, lawyers, athletes, and ministers joined with common murderers, robbers, and rapists to share the wreckage of life. To illustrate my point, I told them the story of an inmate known as "Sheephead."

I had begun to hear tales about Sheephead as soon as I arrived in prison. Inmates and guards spoke of a wild man who was reported to have killed seventeen inmates, and some said he had stabbed thousands of prisoners during the thirty-odd years he had spent in prison. He had also killed one guard and permanently disabled another.

The story was widely circulated that Sheephead chopped an inmate to pieces with a meat cleaver and flushed the parts down the toilet. The guards thought the man had escaped—until they found the skull. It was too large to flush.

Locked in a wing of the prison to minimize the danger to himself as well as to other inmates, Sheephead became a living legend.

Three years passed before I met him. I was being taken to the outside hospital for surgery after severely injuring the little finger on my right hand in a fight.

A guard said, "Wait a minute. Another inmate is going with you."

The door opened and there he stood, the man reputed to be the most violent inmate in the prison. I recognized him immediately because his face did indeed resemble a sheep's head. Every facial bone had been broken in fights. I was frightened of the man.

When the guard shackled my right arm and ankle to Sheephead's left arm and ankle, I worked hard to steady my breathing so he wouldn't sense my fear.

What if he tries to escape and both of us are shot? I thought.

I worried as we were loaded into the prison van for the trip to Talmadge Memorial Hospital in Augusta, Georgia. We rode in silence for a while, and then I found the courage to speak.

"Is it all right if I talk to you?" I said.

"Yeah," growled Sheephead.

"Are the stories I've heard about you really true?"

"You ain't heard nothin' yet," he boasted, and for 110 miles he poured out the story of his life.

He was from a poor family in south Georgia. As a sixteen-year-old boy he had broken into a store to steal a Pepsi and a pack of crackers. He was sentenced to one year in prison and sent to Georgia State Penitentiary. Inmates with a one-year sentence usually are paroled in six months and discharged in eight months.

"I had never been in a fight in my life until I came here," he said. "That first day in prison I was raped by an old inmate. My life was never the same after that. I became a homosexual and a drug addict, but I lived for the day I would be released."

Four months after arriving at the prison, the boy was working on an outside farm detail under the supervision of armed guards. Two old convicts forced him to take part in an escape plot: The men would grab a shotgun from one of the guards, and the teenager would seize the gun from the other guard. Fearing the convicts, the boy complied and grabbed the gun as told, but the other two men did not follow through. In self-defense, the boy shot both guards, killing one and paralyzing the other for life.

"When that guard died, I knew I was through," Sheephead whispered. For a few moments we rode along in silence before the story continued.

After a murder trial, Sheephead was sentenced to die in the electric chair. After he had spent eight-and-a-half years on death row, the governor of Georgia commuted his sentence to life, and he was returned to the inmate population.

No longer frightened, I became fascinated by the old prisoner. As I listened to him and watched him talk, I began to realize that this sick old man was more like a lonely child than a notorious criminal.

When we returned to the prison, Sheephead was locked in a cell in the hospital ward where I worked. Hated by guards and inmates alike, he was a forgotten man. No one cared. He was dying of cancer, although his illness had not yet been diagnosed.

I visited Sheephead daily, often bringing him candy and a Pepsi. As we talked through the bars, I realized that he was so feeble-minded from being beaten in the head that he would kill an inmate if someone merely suggested the man was out to get him. I suspect this accounted for many of the prison killings.

Others saw Sheephead as a violent animal. But I saw him as a broken man who appeared to be 100, though he was only fifty. He loved me because I didn't look down on him. I gave him time and attention, and he returned the friendship by doing whatever I asked. One day, he told me he was planning to kill the doctor.

"He says I just want to go to the hospital to rest. I know I'm dying, but he won't do anything for me. I'm going to kill him," he said. He showed me a knife but didn't explain how he had obtained it.

I begged him not to carry out the plan and promised to see that he received proper medical attention. He agreed. I pleaded his case with the hospital administrator, and tests soon confirmed that he had cancer. As I looked at him, tears filled my eyes and I wondered, *Will that be me someday?*

After spending thirty-four years in prison, Sheephead died. His unwanted body was buried in the prison graveyard. What began with stealing a Pepsi and a pack of crackers ended with terrible waste.

When I finished the story about Sheephead, the teenagers were quiet. I looked at them for a moment, and concluded with this: "You know, kids, the tragedy is not that Sheephead died, but that he never lived. In a few minutes that guard over there will handcuff me and escort me back to the prison. The door will slam, and I'll be there for the rest of my life. It's real, young people, it's real."

The students gave me a standing ovation and wrote scores of letters in the weeks that followed. For the first time in seven years, I realized that I could live a productive life even behind bars. During the next two years I spoke to more than 15,000 students in schools throughout southern Georgia.

Teenagers characteristically support the underdog, and they immediately rallied for me . . . and *against* the guard who waited offstage. He naturally became the butt of my jokes. I asked the students, "If you couldn't identify the guard and me by our clothes, who would you think was the life inmate?" All of them pointed to the guard. Later he warned, "Don't do that. I don't like it."

Whenever I invited questions, hundreds of hands were raised. One girl asked, "How in the world did you get out of prison to come here?" I made up a response.

"Yesterday, this guard was standing on the bank with a shotgun while I was digging a ditch. A little frog came hopping along. I grabbed it and said, 'Frog, I'm going to squash your guts out!' The guard heard me and said, 'Go ahead, convict, but whatever you do to that frog, I'm going to do to you.' I smiled and said, 'Frog, I'm going to kiss your behind and turn you loose!' That's how I became free."

The kids loved my story, but the guard went fuming to the warden and threatened to send me to the hole. But the warden laughed and said, "Go ahead and use that. I like it."

It had been some time since I had heard from my young friend Cliff, and one day his mother came to tell me his basketball team was playing in the state finals that night. She said the game would be broadcast on the radio and he wanted me to listen. I could hardly wait for the game to begin.

Knowing Cliff was just a high-school freshman, I was very proud when they announced his name for the starting lineup. I followed every play as he scored twenty-seven points. With three seconds remaining on the clock, the score was tied. Cliff took a shot and missed, sending the game into overtime. His team eventually won, and he was named most outstanding player. After the game the sports announcer interviewed him.

"Were you nervous taking that shot?" he asked.

"No, sir," Cliff said. "Win or lose, I knew God was with me. You see, I'm a Christian, and everything I do in life, I do for Jesus Christ. I give Him the glory."

As I listened in my prison cell, I realized I'd never given God the glory for my life. The time for that had come.

When Cliff heard that the warden allowed me to speak in area high schools, he insisted that I come to his school. He introduced me to the student body as his friend and talked of the impact I'd had on his life. He said I had made some bad decisions that led me to prison, but I cared about young people. Adding that he loved me and believed in me, he urged the students to listen to what I had to say. When I finished speaking, they gave me a standing ovation. Afterward, Cliff and I played basketball, one-on-one.

By this time, speaking requests were coming from so many schools that the warden decided to charge a fee, hoping to discourage invitations. Still requests poured in, along with letters from hundreds of young people. Imagine, teenagers writing a convict for advice!

Some asked about dating and parent relationships. Others

told of drug and alcohol abuse. A number of girls confided that they were pregnant out of wedlock. Their problems touched my heart, and I devoted all my free time to answering the letters.

I received a letter from a sixteen-year-old girl who said she was a drug addict and dating a married man. She pleaded, "Mr. Morris, you're the only person I can trust. There's no one else. Please help me." I wondered why a teenage girl would think that a man doomed to die in prison was the only person she could trust. Where were her parents? Teachers? Christians who knew her? After we corresponded for about six months, she wrote that she was no longer taking drugs or seeing the married man. She said she had accepted Christ and started going to church. On my knees in that prison cell, I committed my life to helping young people.

Many parents wrote to me. One said, "After hearing your story, my kids promised they would never use drugs. I never dreamed that a convict could help my children. I really appreciate your courage, and I will always be in your debt."

In gratitude for my influence in the schools, the citizens of Douglas, Georgia, invited me to participate in their bicentennial parade, July 4, 1976. I rode in the sheriff's car that led the parade. Although dressed in prison clothes, I felt good realizing that I had done something worthwhile with my life, even under unfortunate circumstances.

Many times on speaking trips outside the prison, I thought about escaping. In fact, I found it very difficult not to escape when faced with such tempting opportunities. But I had given the warden my word, and being a Christian made that commitment very special.

Speaking to young people brought me peace and joy I had never known before. It gave my life a purpose: I was having an impact on others. Although I didn't realize it at that time, God was preparing me for the future.

CHAPTER 11

A BRIEF TASTE
OF FREEDOM

As the years slipped by, I was no closer to freedom than the day I entered the Georgia State Penitentiary to die. However, my family and friends believed in my innocence and continued to fight for my release.

Billy Player, a high-school friend, organized a committee to explore every possible avenue to freedom. His wife, Gloria, served as secretary. The group met with Jimmy Carter, who was governor of Georgia at the time. They went to the scene of the crime and interviewed witnesses, who stated they had never seen me. They spent thousands of dollars and enlisted people all over the country to pray for me.

On September 1, 1976, the warden sent for me to come to the lobby. My two attorneys were on their way to see me, he said. I'd been in prison for seven years and had no money to pay expensive lawyer's fees.

"They aren't my attorneys," I told him.

"There's only one Harold Morris, and they asked to see you."

The men introduced themselves as Danny Falligant and Tom Edenfield, attorneys from Savannah, Georgia. They suggested that we talk privately, and immediately began asking questions.

"How long have you been here?"

"What were the charges against you?"

"Wait a minute!" I said. "What are you doing here?"

"Would you believe that God sent us?"

"If you say so," I said.

They had learned about me through Clebe McClary, but they wanted to see for themselves if I was genuine. I gave them details about the crime, the trial, and the prosecutor. They knew the man.

As they started to leave, Mr. Falligant said, "Harold, if I could do one thing for you, what would it be?"

"Arrange for me to speak to young people. I don't think I'll ever get out of prison, but I have a burden for young people."

Those godly men became a part of my life. They visited me many times and brought their families to meet me. They obtained the warden's permission for me to speak in the high school their children attended.

Joining the fight for my freedom, they contacted the prosecutor. Although he did not favor my parole, he said he would not oppose it.

After trusting Christ, I had written the prosecutor asking his forgiveness for the way I had acted in the courtroom. He sent a harsh reply. As far as I know, he is in private practice, still convinced that I'm another Jesse James.

Time after time I was denied parole. The procedure seemed a mere formality: a written request went to the parole board, and inevitably a letter of rejection came in return. An inmate with a life sentence was allowed only one personal appearance before the board.

On December 8, 1977, I was informed that my hearing before the board would be the following day. My big chance! Unable to sleep that night, I went over the things I would say to convince the board to set me free.

I'll put on a good act . . . cry if necessary. My life is at stake!

After waiting in line all day with about 350 other inmates, I was the last man to be interviewed. The chairman's last name was Morris.

"Maybe we're related," I joked.

"Sit down," he responded gruffly, moving right to the point. "You have two life sentences, and in nine years you've completed all the programs that we have to offer. You've done well. You're not the normal inmate. But we have a problem: Society has not had your body long enough. We feel that you might be in prison another thirty-seven years. What do you have to say?"

My speech went right out the window, along with my heart. I had fostered a hope that he would pat me on the back and say he believed in me. I didn't know how to respond.

"I'm told you're a Christian," the chairman continued. "I don't believe in jailhouse religion, that foot-of-the-cross syndrome. And I don't believe in you. Do you have anything to say?"

"Yes, I do," I said with renewed confidence. "My relationship with Christ is a personal thing between me and the Lord. You cannot know my heart. But let me tell you something, sir. If Jesus Christ wants to free me, He'll open that door. And you can't stop Him!"

"Get out of here," he growled.

The warden was waiting outside. When I told him what had happened, he said, "You idiot! You blew it!"

I repeated my speech. "If Jesus Christ wants to open that door, you can't stop Him."

Lying in my cell, I wept, realizing that I would probably spend the rest of my life in prison. Even so, I had taken a stand for Christ, and He gave me peace.

On previous occasions when I was denied parole, the letter gave various reasons: the severity of the crime, the length of my sentence, or the need for further counseling. My case could be reviewed in a year, but what would change in a year? The severity of the crime would never be altered; a man had been killed. The length of the sentence would never change; the judge had declared two life sentences. The counseling situation would never be any better; most of the counselors were former shotgun guards with no professional training or insight into rehabilitating inmates for a return to society.

I was convinced nothing would change, parole would never become a reality, and I would die in prison.

On January 2, Clebe and his family visited me. A chapel service was hastily arranged, with Clebe preaching, and his wife and two daughters singing. Afterwards, we talked for a while.

"Do you think you'll make parole in March?" he asked.

"No, I really don't."

"I don't understand it," he said. "I was certain that you'd be freed by now. We've done everything we can. Do you have any suggestions?"

I didn't cry in front of him, but my heart was broken again. My freedom hinged on the Lord and my friends, and Clebe had just admitted that they had done everything they knew to do. If my friends had given up, I felt I was through.

Six days later a guard opened the door to my cell about 8 A.M.

"Get your stuff," he said.

Am I going to the hole? Am I being moved to another cell? In the lobby I met the warden.

"Hey, where are you going?" he joked.

"You tell me," I said, puzzled.

"You're leaving the prison," he told me.

"Oh, God! Is my mother dead?"

"I don't know what's going on. The governor teletyped a message here a few minutes ago instructing me to turn you over to an agent from the South Carolina Law Enforcement Division. I thought you might know what it's about."

"Oh, no," I sighed. "My mother's dead!"

About thirty minutes later a man dressed in a suit stepped through the doorway and shook the warden's hand.

"Here he is," the warden said, motioning to me. The man carried no legal papers, and I wore no shackles or handcuffs that cold winter morning as we walked to a car bearing South Carolina license plates. An armed guard watched from the tower.

"Get in front," said the officer. Driving away from the prison, he made a left turn, heading out of state. He offered no explanation.

Am I free? I didn't dare to hope for such a thing.

At first, I was too frightened to speak. But after we had traveled a short distance, I gathered some courage.

"Sir, may I talk to you?"

"Yeah," he said.

I asked his name. It was Mike Carter. I knew the man! His older brother had been involved in sports with me at Winyah. His father was the county sheriff and a close friend of my family. He realized he knew me, too.

"Would you tell me where we're going?" I ventured.

"You're going to Georgetown, South Carolina."

"Is my mother dead?"

"No. You're going to be turned over to Clebe McClary. The governors of South Carolina and Georgia have reached an agreement, based on Clebe's word, allowing you to go home for sixty hours. You're speaking at Clebe's board meeting tomorrow night, and I'll bring you back to the prison on Sunday afternoon. It's the first time I've ever seen anything like this happen."

During the eight-hour drive, I was as excited as a child waiting for Santa Claus! As we came through Charleston, South Carolina, I looked at the historic homes and scenery with the joy of a six-year-old taking his first vacation. A school bus was bogged down in a ditch, and we stopped to help. The bus kicked mud all over me, but that didn't spoil my mood.

My hands are free! My feet are unshackled!

The officer drove to Pawleys Island where Clebe gave him instructions to pick me up at First Baptist Church in Myrtle

Beach at 1 P.M. on Sunday. After explaining the events scheduled for the weekend, Clebe said I could stay with my family.

It seemed like Christmas, being home for the first time in nine years and visiting my mother. My brother Carl and his family had planned a party in my honor; and many of my high-school friends came, along with their wives and children. Carl had even bought new clothes for me—real clothes, without a number on the back!

The restaurant Clebe had rented for the board meeting was packed with men and women who had prayed for me and loved me in Christ long before we met: Bobby Richardson, formerly of the New York Yankees; Tim Foley with the Miami Dolphins; actor Tom Lester, who was Eb on the television show *Green Acres;* James Barker and his wife, Dianne, who would later become coauthor of my life story.

Not knowing what to say, I simply shared the feelings of my heart and thanked everyone for standing with me. When I finished forty-five minutes later, everyone was crying— including me!

Bobby Richardson said, "I love you, Harold, and I believe in you. I'll do anything to help you." That really encouraged me. He even offered to visit the prison to share with the inmates. When he came a few weeks later, many men trusted Christ. Through the friendship of this godly man, I was strengthened time and again.

Charles Reeves, a businessman from Americus, Georgia, was determined to see the governor about my request for parole. Since others had promised miracles they couldn't deliver, I was afraid to put much confidence in his good intentions. In coming days I learned he and my other new friends did not make idle promises; they followed through.

God really blessed the service at First Baptist Church, where Tom Lester and I shared the program. Among those who turned to Christ were two of my nephews.

In the front row sat the law enforcement agent, waiting to take me back into custody. It was both a sad and a happy time. Soon I would again leave my family and friends, old and new, but never had I experienced such a weekend!

Technically I did not have to go back. I hadn't signed extradition papers stating I would return, and being allowed to cross the state line, I was legally freed. I knew the law, but I would not take advantage of the situation, although it was something to think about. If I hadn't been a Christian, I doubt I would have gone back to prison. Then again, if I hadn't been a Christian, I would never have been in that position.

It was late Sunday when we arrived at the prison. I traded my free-world clothes for prison garb and walked to my cell. From my window I watched the officer drive away, and on my knees I thanked God for those sixty hours of freedom—my first lengthy taste of it in more than nine years. While I settled down to the prison routine, my family and friends worked and prayed for divine intervention in a cause that seemed without hope.

CHAPTER 12

FINALLY RELEASED

Winter melted into spring, and as summer gave way to autumn, I supplemented my speaking ministry by participating in a Christmas toy project for underprivileged children. Several prison guards were members of the Jaycees in Reidsville, Georgia, a little town seven miles from the prison. The guards collected broken toys and brought them to me to be repaired. They purchased the mechanical parts I needed, but I used money from my own pocket to pay other inmates to help with the painting and refurbishing of bicycles, tricycles, dolls, small trucks, and toy cars.

When Christmas Eve finally came, the guards loaded the toys into trucks and drove away. How I wished I could see the faces of those happy boys and girls! The joy of completing a worthwhile task made me feel good about myself. The local newspaper even carried my picture and a story about the Joy Toys project.

As I lay on my bunk that Christmas Day, I remembered an earlier Christmas when I was a newcomer to Georgia State Penitentiary. At the time, I owned nothing but the same loafers I had worn coming in, and I traded those for six Pepsi Colas. I no longer wanted beautiful women and fancy cars. A Pepsi would make my day!

I set the drinks on the window hoping they would be chilled by the freezing air outside. Lying on my bunk, considering how low I had come in life, I sipped those tepid drinks and moaned, "What a Christmas . . . what a Christmas!"

How my life changed when the Holy Child of Christmas became the center of my existence! What a Christmas indeed! Soon the holiday season faded into the routine of prison life. About 7 P.M. on January 6, 1978, a guard came to my cell and unlocked the door.

"Get ready," he said. "You're going outside the institution."

In the lobby, I was met by one of the counselors.

"You're coming with me," he said, offering no further explanation.

Leaving the prison at night was highly unusual, and I wasn't even handcuffed. The counselor drove to Reidsville, parked at a restaurant, and escorted me inside a banquet room. I recognized the sheriff, the mayor, and several prison guards who were members of the Jaycees. Their wives were also there. I had no idea what I was doing at the banquet, and I wasn't excited about wearing my prison clothes. After a while, I thought I'd figured it out.

The counselor brought me to clean up! I surmised. *After the banquet, I'm expected to wash dishes and sweep the floor!*

He showed me where to sit and told me to take a plate.

Boy, this is nice, I thought. *At least I get to eat.*

During the meal, many of the townspeople came to speak with me. After several presentations were made to various men, I realized this was the Jaycees Awards Banquet. Finally, the counselor who brought me addressed the group. He discussed the Joy Toys program, mentioning the hours spent preparing the toys, and the delighted children who had received them.

"Ladies and gentlemen," he said, "in recognition of his contribution to the youth of this community, we are presenting the Jaycees Presidential Award of Honor to Harold Morris."

The crowd burst into applause as I tried to grasp the

reality, wondering if I would awake in my prison cell and discover it was only a dream. As the applause died, the counselor asked me to speak. I looked into the faces of prison guards. It was a rare thing for an inmate to have a good relationship with guards and rarer still to be honored in the presence of their wives and dignitaries of the community. They accepted my thanks without knowing all that was going on in my heart.

Imagine, such an honor for a convict! There's hope for me. My dad was wrong—I can be somebody! Thank you, God!

But realizing that I *was* somebody—and being a Christian—did nothing to diminish my desire to be released from prison! I was very distraught, longing to be free yet unable to hope. Finally I made a decision: If I didn't make parole by April 6—Easter Sunday—I would escape.

The warden had promised me a sixty-hour pass for the weekend. I told no one of my plan except the two people to be involved in the drama—my brother, who would pick me up at the prison, and a friend, who would give me enough money to leave the country. Both wanted me freed by legal means, but they were convinced, as I was, that my chances were running out. Rather than see me die in prison, they were willing to take a risk.

Using a phony passport, I could travel anywhere in the world before being missed at the prison. I knew it was wrong, but there seemed no other alternative. Fortunately, before I had the chance to implement my plan, God intervened. On March 1, a letter arrived from the State Board of Prison and Parole. Trembling, I opened it. On the following page is a reproduction of that correspondence which represented my freedom . . . at last!

Freedom! God used the efforts of my family and friends, but I'm certain that prayer is the reason I'm a free man today. I was allowed a five-minute phone call to share the good news with my brother Carl.

March 14—it was two weeks away! But it seemed like two

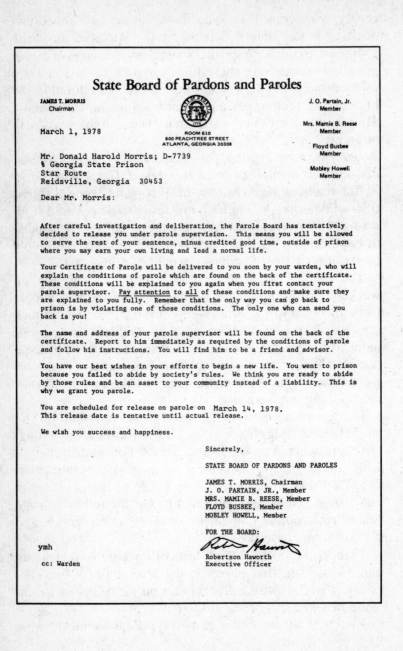

State Board of Pardons and Paroles

JAMES T. MORRIS
Chairman

March 1, 1978

ROOM 610
800 PEACHTREE STREET
ATLANTA, GEORGIA 30308

J. O. Partain, Jr.
Member

Mrs. Mamie B. Reese
Member

Floyd Busbee
Member

Mobley Howell
Member

Mr. Donald Harold Morris; D-7739
% Georgia State Prison
Star Route
Reidsville, Georgia 30453

Dear Mr. Morris:

After careful investigation and deliberation, the Parole Board has tentatively decided to release you under parole supervision. This means you will be allowed to serve the rest of your sentence, minus credited good time, outside of prison where you may earn your own living and lead a normal life.

Your Certificate of Parole will be delivered to you soon by your warden, who will explain the conditions of parole which are found on the back of the certificate. These conditions will be explained to you again when you first contact your parole supervisor. Pay attention to all of these conditions and make sure they are explained to you fully. Remember that the only way you can go back to prison is by violating one of those conditions. The only one who can send you back is you!

The name and address of your parole supervisor will be found on the back of the certificate. Report to him immediately as required by the conditions of parole and follow his instructions. You will find him to be a friend and advisor.

You have our best wishes in your efforts to begin a new life. You went to prison because you failed to abide by society's rules. We think you are ready to abide by those rules and be an asset to your community instead of a liability. This is why we grant you parole.

You are scheduled for release on parole on March 14, 1978.
This release date is tentative until actual release.

We wish you success and happiness.

                                        Sincerely,

                                        STATE BOARD OF PARDONS AND PAROLES

                                        JAMES T. MORRIS, Chairman
                                        J. O. PARTAIN, JR., Member
                                        MRS. MAMIE B. REESE, Member
                                        FLOYD BUSBEE, Member
                                        MOBLEY HOWELL, Member

                                        FOR THE BOARD:

ymh
                                        Robertson Haworth
cc: Warden   Executive Officer

years. I was afraid to leave my cell. I might get into trouble . . . or be killed. Not wanting to take any chances, I stayed by myself and prayed as never before.

I was excited yet frightened about going into a world I didn't know. But I was convinced about one thing: It would be an absolutely wonderful life serving the Lord in the free world!

A job awaited me at the Brookland Boys Home in Orangeburg, South Carolina. My parole officer explained that I would be assigned to another officer in Orangeburg, and many rules accompanied my freedom. I would not be allowed to leave the Orangeburg city limits; I couldn't even leave my residence before 6 A.M. or stay out past midnight. It seemed I needed permission from my parole officer for everything except breathing! To buy a house or car or to marry required approval. Because I had been convicted of a felony, the rights of U.S. citizenship were not restored. That didn't matter. . . . I'd be free!

On March 13—my last day in prison—I went to see several old friends. I visited with one man who had spent forty-seven years in prison. Oh, the tragedy of a wasted life! There were many hugs along with prayers that I would have a successful life on the outside.

That afternoon, I looked up to see Cliff approaching me. He had heard that I was to be paroled the following day. He reaffirmed his love and thanked me for being the brother he'd always wanted. Then he promised to visit me at the Boys Home.

We were both emotional when we shook hands and said our goodbyes. Parting with friends is never easy.

It was particularly difficult to leave my cellmate, Big Willie. That night in our cell we talked about my new life in the free world, and Willie said, "I love you, Harold."

"Brother, I love you, too!"

There was no sleep for me that night. Finally, morning came. Fully awake at 5 A.M., I lay in bed thinking about what was ahead. *In just three hours, I'll be leaving the prison.*

At 8 o'clock, a guard will unlock the door and I'll be a free man—for the first time in almost ten years. I was frightened to death. But I knew that when I walked out that door, Jesus Christ would walk with me. I knew that supportive family members and friends would be waiting. More than anything in the world, I wanted them to see my changed life. I wanted Jesus to be visible in everything I said and did.

Through the window, I could see the sunrise. I held those cold, unfriendly bars and watched the earth take on a golden glow as I tried to remember when I first came to the prison. It seemed so long ago!

Overcome with emotion, I fell to my knees and thanked God—for my life, my freedom, my family, and my friends. I thanked Him for the new life He was giving to me. Above all, I thanked Him for saving my soul, for establishing the relationship with Him in my heart, and for flooding my life with peace and joy.

On my knees I was reminded of the instructions that Jesus gave His disciples. His words recorded by Matthew were, "Go therefore and make disciples of all the nations."[1] Mark heard Him say, "Go into all the world and preach the gospel to every creature."[2] The command in Luke was, "Repentance and remission of sins should be preached in His name to all nations, beginning at Jerusalem. And you are witnesses of these things."[3] These words were recorded by John: "As the Father has sent Me, I also send you."[4]

Christ promised on the day of His ascension, "But you will receive power when the Holy Spirit has come upon you, and you will be witnesses to Me in Jerusalem, and in Judea and Samaria, and to the ends of the earth."

In that prison cell on March 14, 1978, I made a commitment that set the direction of my remaining life.

Father, as I leave here today, I will make young people my Jerusalem; prisons, my Judea; churches, my Samaria. I will go anywhere on earth to serve You.

---

1. Matthew 28:19.   2. Mark 16:15.   3. Luke 24:47.   4. John 20:21

What a joy it would be to tell others about the Lord Jesus, who loved me enough to give His life that I might be free from the power of sin and death! How blessed I felt, thinking about the eternal and abundant life I'd found in Him!

Suddenly, I heard footsteps and the sound of keys. The guard who unlocked the door said nothing as he led me to the building where the final paperwork was done before inmates left the institution. Also being paroled were two inmates whom I'd never met. Even though I'd been in prison for many years, I knew only the inmates who worked with me or lived in the dorm or served time in the hole with me. The three of us talked of our plans as we waited for the procession to be completed.

"We've got some clothes for you," said an old guard, handing each of us an outdated polyester suit and a pair of white socks. He then offered each of us a bus ticket to our destination and a check for $25—meager wages for ten years of work.

"I don't need any of that. My family is coming," I explained.

"Ain't nobody coming to get you," he snarled. "You'd better take this bus ticket and these clothes, and get out of here."

"My family is coming," I repeated. "They care about me. They'll be here."

The other two inmates changed clothes and boarded a bus for a little town seven miles away. As I watched them leave, I began to imagine what would happen if I were the typical inmate.

I accept the suit, the $25 check, and the bus ticket. Arriving in a strange town, I have no identification. After all, I'm not a citizen of the United States. Cashing the check proves to be very difficult, but finally it is approved. After buying three meals, I'm almost broke—just enough left for a couple of beers. A beer joint is the one place I should never be! Now I'm high, but broke. I sleep on the sidewalk and start the day looking for work. When the prospective employer asks for *three references, I name the warden and two inmates. He threatens to call the sheriff to lock me up.*

In my imagination, I continue the scenario . . . *I turn and look at the man who could have been me—without friends, without money, without hope. How long would it be until I hurt someone?* At that moment I understood why men return to prison. They can't manage their lives. Living is hard on the outside, and a life of crime is all they have known. At least in the institution, they are among men who profess to be friends, and they receive free meals. No wonder the return rate is eighty-five percent.

As the mental picture of "Harold Morris, the typical inmate" faded, I began to pace the floor . . . 8:15 and my family had not arrived.

"I told you nobody cares," the guard reminded me. "You'd better take this suit and get out of here. There ain't nobody coming to get you, you animal."

"Not everybody hates me," I said. "I have people who care." By 8:30 my family still had not come, but I wasn't worried. Some problem had caused the delay. I knew they would come; they had invested five years in my life.

Finally, at 8:45 A.M. a van pulled up in front of the prison, bringing my brother Carl and other members of my family, along with several friends. I thanked God for them, knowing that no other inmate had ever been met by more caring, supportive people.

Carl hurried through the prison door, explaining the motel where they stayed in Savannah had failed to make the wake-up call as requested. He handed me a pair of pants and a shirt. The average man attaches little significance to changing clothes, but I was hardly average. I was Convict 62345 becoming a free man!

I accepted the $25 check for nine-and-a-half years of labor, representing less than a penny a day. At 8:52 A.M., after a 3,500-day interruption in my life, I walked out of prison, a free man!

A brilliant sun peeked through the trees as I stepped out-

side and looked around. This gorgeous day was unlike the
morning I arrived at Georgia State Penitentiary. The threatening fence was there, of course, and the ominous tower
with rifle-ready guards. Standing in the very place where I
had stood that day in shackles and gazed at the front of the
prison, I remembered the words spoken by the guard: "You
will die here. You will never be free again."

But another voice was speaking to my heart on this day—
the word of the Lord to Abraham in Genesis 18:14, "Is there
anything too hard for the Lord? How great God is! Nothing
is too difficult for Him!"

The earth was bursting with overtures of spring and my
heart with immense gratitude as I knelt in the shadow of the
guard tower, thanking God for a new beginning. Stepping
into the van, I wondered if the prison nightmare really had
ended or if parole were only a dream.

Seven miles from the prison in the town of Reidsville, a
parade happened to be under way.

"A parade! You've overdone it," I teased, knowing it was
merely a coincidence. The laughter of merry hearts was like
medicine healing my tattered soul.

When we reached Claxton after traveling just twenty
miles, I suggested that we stop to eat. I've never had a better
meal than the breakfast I ate that morning at Mr. Roger's
Restaurant. I don't know if it was the taste of the food or
the taste of freedom.

After eating, I turned to my brother. "Where's the rest-
room?" I asked. "For nearly ten years I haven't gone to the
john without someone watching!"

We drove on to South Carolina for the highlight of my
release—holding my dear mother in my arms and telling her
I loved her. This time I didn't hear the trained dogs barking
in the distance or feel the shame of wearing prison clothes.
When I looked into my mother's face, I finally understood
how much she had suffered because of my suffering. I realized that *her* prison term ended with mine.

As we talked, I found the courage to ask about her re-

lationship with Christ. For years I had wanted to know if
the person I loved more than anyone else on earth would
be in heaven some day. Momma described in detail the night
she trusted Christ during a revival service when I was twelve
years old. She wasn't offended that I asked. In fact, she was
just extremely grateful that I cared. After my father's death,
she had married a fine Christian man, Bryant Wiggins, Sr.,
for whom I have a deep love and respect.

Within twenty-four hours after my release from prison, I
had to check in with my parole officer in Orangeburg. To
my surprise, the officer was a stunning lady.

"Ma'am, I haven't seen a woman in nine-and-a-half
years," I said. "You're beautiful! I don't know the rules, but
I'd be glad to report to you every day!"

Laughing, she said, "We're going to get along just fine."
She explained that I would report to her in person once a
month as well as submit written reports monthly. She gave
me permission to spend a week with my family before starting to work at the Boys Home. As I left, she reminded me
that I was not a citizen of the United States, that I couldn't
vote, and that I couldn't own property without her permission. Those restrictions didn't discourage me. I had the
mighty Christ in my heart, a loving family and friends, and
an understanding and supportive parole officer to help
smooth the way.

I had never been to the Boys Home, but some of the
youngsters had sent letters to the prison. When I arrived,
the boys were waiting for me. Large yellow ribbons were
tied around the pecan trees, and a big sign announced, "Welcome home, Mr. Morris." I cried, realizing that here I would
be loved and needed.

My responsibilities included coaching and counseling the
boys, who were ages eight to eighteen and from varied back-
grounds. Some were orphans, some had been abused and
neglected by their parents, some had been kicked out to
roam the streets, and some were from broken homes. They
were exactly what I needed. Being outcasts themselves, they

wouldn't look down on me. I learned a great deal as those kids worked their way into my heart.

One unforgettable eight-year-old really won me over. Jerry had been abused by his parents. His vision was poor, and he spoke with difficulty. His mental ability also appeared limited, and the kids picked on him constantly. Once, Jerry and several others attended a large summer camp. When I stopped by to check on them, I noticed that all the kids from other places were eating snacks, but my boys had no money for such treats. I bought them each a candy bar and a soft drink and left some money in an account for each boy. As I started to leave, little Jerry came running up to me.

"Mr. Harold, I know why you bought us that candy and pop," he said.

"Why?" I responded.

"Because you love us," he said, wrapping his arms around my legs.

I turned my face so that he couldn't see the tears. That small boy—so physically and mentally limited that he could hardly express himself—was the only boy who showed gratitude. He gave more love than all the others! I have never forgotten Jerry or the lesson I learned from him: Never judge a person by what he appears to be; in the hands of God, his potential is limitless.

CHAPTER 13

ADJUSTMENTS

I was unprepared to reenter the society I had left a decade ago. Times had changed, but I had not changed with them. In the area of politics I was well informed, having read a great deal while in prison. Most inmates don't bother. I once asked an old prisoner, "Who's the President of the United States?" Scratching his head in thought, he replied, "George Wallace?" I walked on wondering, *Is that going to be me one day?*

Contact with high-school students through the speaking program in prison had kept me informed about teen problems and attitudes, but the change in moral values came as a surprise. I had not expected to find such widespread immorality. In the area of male-female relationships, it was a whole new ballgame.

The openness of homosexuals gave me another jolt. Although I had lived with them in prison and despised their sin, I was not aware of the rights they had gained on the outside.

Freedom gave me an appreciation for the things that many people take for granted. What a joy it was to talk on the telephone! During my first five years in prison, I did not make or receive one phone call, and for the last four-and-a-half years, my calls were limited. In the free world I could pick up the phone every day and tell someone, "I love you!"

At first people seemed to have a problem communicating with me. "What do you think?" they would ask, in an attempt to draw me into the conversation. They didn't realize that in prison, I didn't grow as they had grown. My life had stopped many years earlier, leaving a tremendous void. I could contribute only memories.

Making decisions proved very difficult for a while. In prison, my life had been managed for me. I was told when to go to bed, when to get up, when and where to work, and when to eat. Even the amount of food had been predetermined and served on my plate. Ordering from a menu in the free world was a frightening experience. Salad bars were terrifying!

I happened to be with friends in a shopping mall in Charleston, South Carolina, when I found something unbelievable—rows of restaurants! I went door to door, ordering a little at each. After sampling the fare at half the restaurants, I decided to wait until the next day to try the others. I'd already made a pig out of myself! To be able to eat anything I wanted seemed overwhelming. I ate every meal as if it would be my last. The result was a weight gain that eventually affected my health before being brought under control.

Inflation offered another big surprise. Fifty cents for a Pepsi Cola. One cost fifteen cents when I went to prison. All I wanted was some refreshment. I wasn't interested in buying stock in the company!

My employer signed a bank note so I could purchase an automobile. Designs had changed so drastically that I hardly knew a Volkswagen from a Cadillac. Passing a junk yard, I marvelled at some nine-year-old models I'd never even seen.

Buying clothes embarrassed me because I knew nothing about styles. The sales clerks really had a field day.

Occasionally, a very simple thing proved to be a large challenge. Some friends hosted a party for me, and I went to the kitchen for a drink of water. I twisted those fancy knobs in every direction, but the water just wouldn't come. When I heard their laughter, my friends worried that I might be embarrassed. Someone whispered, "He doesn't even know how to turn on the faucet." I really wasn't embarrassed. God has a way of helping us make adjustments, and before long I was back into the routine.

The adjustments to a life of freedom almost overcame me. But the Lord used the fellowship of His church to bridge the gap between the past and the present. I was baptized at Harmony Church in Sumter, South Carolina. Rev. Bob Norris, former Yankee Bobby Richardson, and other godly men took me under their wing and discipled me.

One recurring theme came up again and again as I studied my Bible and listened to the sermons: forgiveness. As I grew in the Lord and learned what the Bible says about forgiveness, I realized that telling a person he has been forgiven helps finalize it.

About two months after being released from prison, I decided to try to find the men who had betrayed me. One of the parole rules stated that I was never to have contact with an ex-offender, and I had intended to honor it. Knowing the kind of men Jack and Danny were, I feared they might try to kill me.

Nonetheless, I felt it was important to bring closure to the problems between us.

After numerous phone calls to mutual acquaintances, I finally located Danny in North Carolina. His wife answered. When Danny came to the phone, he said, "Who is this?"

"Don't you recognize my voice?"

"No, I don't think I do."

"Does the name Harold Morris mean anything to you?"

"Where are you?" he gasped in fright.

On the day of my conviction, I had promised to kill him, and I'd sent word from prison that I intended to keep my word. I thought about saying, "Turn around and look through the window. There's a gun pointed at you." Instead, I replied, "Don't worry, I'm in South Carolina."

"Harold, I'm sorry! Forgive me! They said if I tried to help you, I'd go to prison forever!"

"Listen," I interrupted his explanation. "I just called to tell you that I'm a Christian and to ask you to forgive me for wanting to kill you. I love you."

He began to cry and asked me to come see him.

"Hey, I said I *love* you. I didn't say I trust you!"

I asked how to reach Jack. Danny gave me a Florida number, but when I called, it had been disconnected. I called Danny again and asked him to tell Jack that I tried to contact him to say I had forgiven him. I never heard from Jack and I've had no further contact with Danny.

Forgiveness healed the wounds, and telling Danny sealed forever what God had done in my heart. I would love to see those men today to share the hope and joy I've found in Christ.

Meanwhile, I continued to receive numerous requests to share my testimony in churches and schools around the country. The men who were discipling me—Pastor Norris and Bobby Richardson—urged me to attend Bible college to become better grounded in the Word of God. Preparation came before performance, they stressed.

The thought of going back to college held about as much appeal as going back to prison. I rebelled against the idea. Seeing that my friends wouldn't give up, I finally sent an application to a school in South Carolina, even though my heart wasn't in it. A letter from the college president stated that I was being rejected because I was divorced. I sent a reply: "No problem, I'll get married." Comedians weren't welcome, either, I discovered.

The rejection did not come as a disappointment to me because I had applied under pressure from friends. Although I needed Bible teaching, I wasn't ready for the discipline that would be required.

My pastor contacted one of his friends, who happened to be president of Southeastern Bible College in Birmingham, Alabama. The school's policy stated that a person who had been convicted of a felony could not enroll until one year after release from prison. I had been free only ten months, but the president agreed to accept me on the recommendation of Norris and Richardson

Another hurdle had to be overcome: My parole officer had to grant permission for me to leave South Carolina. Reviewing the sequence of events, she pointed out that permission was needed not only from the state of South Carolina, but also from Georgia, where I was paroled, and from Alabama, where I would be living. She advised me to forget Bible college.

I assured my pastor that there was no need to pursue the idea. Confidently, he remarked, "It will be interesting to see how God works this out."

"You don't understand," I said, "He just worked it out!"

"Oh, no, He didn't. The college has accepted you, even though the semester has already started. You must leave this weekend and begin classes on Monday. Let's pray about it," he urged.

Begin classes on Monday? It was Friday afternoon! I paid another visit to my parole officer.

"Ma'am, please tell me why it is so difficult for someone to study the Word of God. All I want is a chance to learn, but that has been denied. Would you explain why?"

Thoughtful for a moment, she began to write.

"Here," she said, handing a form to me. "This is a temporary traveling permit. If any law enforcement officer questions you, tell him to call me. You can see a parole officer in Birmingham. I'll start the paperwork, but it could be months before permission is granted. I'm putting my job on the line, but I don't care. Go to that Bible college and study the Word of God."

I thanked her with a big hug and left to tell my friends what God had done.

One large reality remained: I still had no money for tuition. Nevertheless, on Sunday night I was on my way to Birmingham, accompanied by Bob Norris and another friend, Mike Blake. After they helped me settle into a room on campus, I drove them to the airport. Before boarding the plane, my pastor handed me an envelope which Barnes Boyle, Jr., a Sumter businessman, had asked him to deliver. Inside was a check for $2,000 . . . God's abundant provision!

I'd been on campus for only two days when Dewey Crim, a banker from Birmingham, invited me to stay with his family. Several months earlier he had made a trip to South Carolina to meet me after hearing a tape of my testimony. His wife, son, and twin daughters agreed with him about asking me to share their home. Through the relationship with that deeply committed Christian family, God enriched my life. I found it difficult to leave after my first semester of school, but God had made it financially possible for me to rent an apartment. He marvelously supplied my needs through speaking engagements every weekend, along with support from Harmony Church as well as other churches and individuals.

Going to college after nearly ten years in prison can only be described as a growing experience. Besides being there somewhat against my will, I was twice the age of most of the students on campus. However, they accepted me immediately. In one course I sat beside a pretty girl who appeared to be about eighteen years old. In the middle of class I wrote a note to her.

"It says in Genesis that woman was made from man's rib. If that's true, you're most definitely a prime rib!" She and the other students fell in love with me.

On Monday nights a group of my friends gathered in the cafeteria to eat and fellowship. Fascinated by my background, they listened to prison stories for hours. They not only confided their problems to me, but also shared the concerns of my heart. How exciting it was being used of God to minister to each other.

Several students witnessed in prisons with me and helped with a weekly Bible study I organized at a correctional institution for children and youth, located near the college. On the first night of our study, fifty-four of the seventy-four boys and girls at the facility trusted Christ. Seeing those youngsters come to Jesus helped me and my college friends grow in faith.

Everyone on campus bent over backwards to help me. James Raiford, who was the dean of faculty as well as an outstanding teacher, became a devoted friend. We attended ball games, ate meals, and prayed together. Surely it was divinely arranged for this godly man to disciple me.

I had never been a good student, and attending college didn't automatically change that. Before my first test I studied all night, and when the grades were recorded, I had a D-minus.

Discouragement walked me to my car and talked with me as I sat on a hill overlooking the city of Birmingham. All I could think was, *You're not ready for this. You can't do college work. You'd better quit before you fail.*

Feeling the sting of tears, I opened my Bible and found Joshua 1:9 staring me in the face: "Have I not commanded you? Be strong and of good courage; do not be afraid, nor be dismayed, for the Lord your God is with you wherever you go."

Sinking to my knees beside the car, I prayed, "Father, thank you for my life, for my freedom, and for the opportunity to attend Bible college. I'm not very bright, but I want to learn. I'm going back into that classroom, and I'm going to graduate. I might not make good grades, but I'll learn more than any one else."

The degree I was studying for, a Bachelor of Arts in Christian Ministries, required one year of Greek. The course could be condensed into two months of intensive study during the summer—four hours in class, five days a week. With fear and trembling, I enrolled. But only because I had no choice.

I'll never forget my first day or my initial impression of the teacher. I immediately lost respect for him because of his physical appearance. His legs were so pitifully entangled that he had not walked without the aid of crutches during his thirty-three years. He also suffered from a hearing loss and blindness in one eye. I assumed that a man with such severe disabilities could not teach effectively. The professor faced the class of nine students and made an unusual request.

"I live with my parents in Trustville, which is about twenty-five miles each way," he said. "I can't drive, and I wonder if some of you would pray about giving me a ride every day."

That should be good for a "B!" The thought crossed my mind with mock seriousness. In any case, I volunteered to pick him up every morning, even though it would require getting up earlier than usual. It seemed the least I could do for someone in his condition. I didn't realize that God was working. Another student offered to drive him home. After the transportation was arranged, he settled down to business with this introduction: "Class, when you look at me, many of you don't have much respect for me because I'm not much to look at." Before the tears could spill, I had asked God to forgive me.

"Although I'm handicapped, Jesus Christ is on the throne of my life," he continued. "When you question my qualifications, you'll find that I've graduated first in every class that I've taken, both here and at seminary. I've studied Greek for most of my life. In fact, it *is* my life. I can't preach or travel, but I can teach Greek, and I'm going to teach you more than you've ever learned in your life. You're my legs to carry the gospel to the world. Get ready, because you'll have to work as you've never worked before." The class stood and burst into applause.

Other students had warned me that Greek was a difficult language, and several who were better students than I were grateful to shoot for a "D" in the class. But after that emotional first day, the "C" that I'd set as my goal didn't seem high enough. I decided I was willing to pay the price for an "A." For those eight weeks in the summer of my junior year, I lived and breathed Greek, and I earned the "A!"

During our drives to school, the Greek professor and I

exchanged life stories. His physical disabilities were caused by complications that arose during his mother's pregnancy, but he certainly was not limited in intellectual ability. I grew to love him, and one day I asked his forgiveness for my judgmental attitude. Through him I learned a valuable lesson—that God alone can judge. I need to be concerned only that when I stand before my Lord, I'll hear Him say, "Well done, my good and faithful servant."

The Greek professor was an important teacher in my learning process, but God designed my circumstances so carefully that other divine appointments also took place. One of my fellow classmates planted his footprints firmly in my heart, and his influence changed forever the way I looked at life.

I had heard of William Russell Moore months before we met. In almost every class, someone requested prayer for him because he was hospitalized with cancer in Houston, Texas. I wrote to him, saying I'd heard many good things about him and promising to pray for him. I also added a few notes about myself.

In the fall of 1979, six weeks after having his left leg amputated below the hip, Russell was back on campus wearing an artificial leg and the warmest smile I'd ever seen. He carried his textbooks and Bible under one arm and a black walking cane in the other hand. I introduced myself to him.

"So you're Harold Morris!" he exclaimed. "Thanks for your encouraging letters. They helped." He smiled, cocked his head and stared at me for a few seconds. Then he nodded slightly and said, "You've gone through quite a bit yourself."

Encouraged by his warmth, I found myself spending a lot of time with him. We shared our deepest dreams in the days that followed, and I marveled at the young man's courage and determination to accomplish what he believed was God's will for him.

"Harold," he told me, "God has given me a deep love for the Jewish people, and I want very much to spend the rest

of my life in Israel. Before I got sick, I had planned to enroll
in Hebrew University in Jerusalem. I worked hard to earn
the money, and then the very day of the trip, I got sick."
He thumped his artificial leg. "Cancer in my left knee. But
the doctors think they got it all, and as soon as I'm strong
again, I'm going to Israel. And I want you to come with
me."

I shared Russell's dream of traveling to Israel, and I had
a passport. My problem was that as a convicted felon I was
not supposed to leave the country.

One day Russell returned to the doctor for a routine
check-up, and X-rays revealed a suspicious spot on one lung.
Two weeks later he saw the doctor again, and afterward he
came straight to my apartment.

"What did the doctor say?" I asked as he stood in the
doorway, supported by his walking cane.

"Brother," he smiled, "get your Bible."

I brought it from the bedroom, and Russell sat on the
couch with it, underlining a passage from the Psalms. When
he had finished, he handed it to me, and I read what he had
marked:

"So teach us to number our days,
That we may gain a heart of wisdom.
Return, O Lord!
How long?
And have compassion on Your servants.
Oh, satisfy us early with Your mercy,
That we may rejoice and be glad all our days!
Make us glad according to the days in
  which You have afflicted us,
And the years in which we have seen evil.
Let Your work appear to Your servants,
And Your glory to their children.
And let the beauty of the Lord our God be upon us,
And establish the work of our hands for us;
Yes, establish the work of our hands."
—Psalm 90:12–17

Puzzled, I looked up at him.

"That's you and me, brother," he said matter-of-factly.

"What did the doctor say?" I asked again.

"Brother, if the doctors know what they're talking about, I have twelve days to live."

CHAPTER 14

ANGELS, BROTHER, ANGELS

I stared at him, unable to absorb the news. Receiving two life sentences was nothing compared to this. Twelve days to live!

What does one say to someone who learns he is dying when he has just begun? As I looked at Russell—a young man who was sold out to Christ, who studied the Word of God every day, who lived to witness—I could think of nothing to say.

Finally, I found my voice. "Russell," I asked softly, "what are you going to do?"

"I want to do three things before I die," he said. "First, I'll continue my Bible college training because the Word of God is my life. Second, I'd give anything to go with you to a prison and hold a service for the inmates. Third, I must go to Israel. God has called me to that country to witness to the Jews. I want to die there."

Russell attended classes for another week. Growing weaker each day, he asked me to see if the college president would arrange for him to speak to the student body before returning to the hospital. The chapel was packed with students and faculty as Russell challenged us never to forsake God's calling.

"Some of you are playing games with God," he said.

"When you came here you had a vision and a purpose. But you've lost that direction. You know that you're playing games. It's time to get serious with God."

When he finished, every student and faculty member stood with tear-stained faces. The ovation was for the living Christ, whom Russell had chosen to honor, whether in life or in death. His mother and I helped him leave the stage, and that night he entered the hosptial to die.

I visited Russell every day. At his bedside, I'd pretend to search the covers, exclaiming, "There's a leg missing! I think you have cancer!"

He'd laugh and say, "You're different. I really feel comfortable around you." Sometimes in the middle of the night he'd call saying, "Brother, I need to see you. Come minister to me."

Twelve days passed, yet he clung to life. His mother stayed by his side as he underwent chemotherapy and suffered the notorious side effects. He lost his hair and a great deal of weight. At times, visitors were restricted when his white blood count dropped, leaving him susceptible to infection. One day as I started into his room, he stopped me.

"Hold it! My white blood count is down to 800. Brother, before you take another step, please pray that it will double. I believe God will do it if we just pray." The next morning he called me.

"Hey, brother, it didn't double. It tripled!"

During the next few weeks, Russell was in and out of the hospital many times. Although he struggled with pain, he never lost his faith, his fervor for witnessing, or his sense of humor. I was already grieving for him, and one day as we drove through Birmingham, he teased me out of my somber mood.

"Why are you so quiet? Don't be glum. Listen, brother. So what if I die? Just think, I'll be in heaven! If you have a flat down here, and you're too lazy to change it, I could send a couple of angels down to help. And another thing, I'll have seniority over you when you get there."

Hardly a day went by that he didn't beg me to go to Israel.

"Russell, I can't go. You know I'm on parole. Get your dad or someone else."

"You're it," he said. "You're the only one who can pull it off."

Even if I dared risk violating parole, I didn't have the money to make the trip. Russell had already thought of that. He had an insurance check that would cover most of the cost. Torn between what I wanted to do and what I could do, I prayed. On one of my visits to the hospital, I met Russell's physician.

"How's he doing?" I asked.

"Not very well," he said. "The right lung is completely gone, and only one-third of the left one remains. I don't know how he's breathing. I'd give him no more than four days to live." I walked to my friend's bedside.

"Russell, if you knew that you only had four days to live, what would you do with your life?"

"I'd go to Israel. I want to die in that country."

"Let's go!" I said. *God, it's up to You,* I prayed.

"I love you, brother!" he said, reaching up to hug my neck. Immediately his health began to improve. He called for the doctor and bargained, "If you'll let me go home, I'll eat vegetables and get strong. I'm going to spend Christmas in Israel!"

The doctor loved Russell as a son and reluctantly agreed to his making the trip. "People will call me a fool for letting him go," he sighed "And they'll call you a fool for going," he said to me.

"They've called me a fool all my life, but I don't care," I said. "I've made my decision."

He gave detailed instructions about Russell's medical care and asked if I could administer the injection every five hours.

I assured him I knew how to use needles. I had used drugs before I became a Christian, and had given injections to other inmates. He typed a letter authorizing me to carry the drugs and syringes.

"Give this to the captain of the plane and to any authorities who question you," he said. "If a problem arises, tell them to call me collect. I'll be praying for you."

Not all my friends at the Bible college endorsed our plans.

"You will violate parole by leaving the country," a professor pointed out. "And Russell is not physically able to make an eleven-day trip. If that boy dies, you'll be locked up. We don't want that to happen."

I figured that if God hadn't wanted me to go, I would not have received a passport. But I'd obtained one months earlier—before Russell even suggested the trip.

Whenever I discussed my passport with Russell, he smiled knowingly.

"Angels, brother," he said merrily. "Angels!"

The next morning Russell's parents drove us to the airport. Although they realized that they might never see their son alive again, they understood the desire that consumed him, and they did not try to discourage him. As I pushed his wheelchair up the ramp at the Birmingham airport that sunny Sunday morning in December of 1979, his mother hugged us both and said, "Take care of him, Harold."

"We'll be back," I said, trying to appear confident.

During our flight to New York and our eleven-hour flight to Israel, Russell witnessed to anyone who would listen. Most of the passengers were Jewish, and they were drawn to him, curious about his reasons for traveling while so obviously ill. Even flight attendants knelt by his side as he shared God's Word and his reasons for going to Israel. After finishing he'd say, "You haven't heard anything yet. Listen to his story." I'd give them round two! At one point during our trip I felt a nudge on my shoulder and turned to find a flight attendant in tears.

"Sir, I'm thankful to God that you and that young boy were on this plane," she said. "I was ready to divorce my husband, but because of that young man, I have recommitted myself to Christ and to my marriage. I had to thank you. Please look after him."

We rented a car as soon as we arrived in Tel Aviv. The doctor had cautioned me that the slightest exercise would exhaust Russell, decreasing his chances for survival. He had stressed that driving was out of the question. But as soon as we rented a car, Russell announced, "I want to drive."

"Take over," I said, and he headed toward Jerusalem forty miles away. We were barely a mile out of Tel Aviv when we passed two young hitchhikers—girls dressed in military uniforms. Russell stopped, and the soldiers climbed into the backseat. One spoke English fluently, having graduated from Boston University. She listened as Russell shared his faith. When we reached her home in Jerusalem, she gave us her phone number and suggested we have dinner together after we had toured some of the cities.

Russell and I found a room at the Moriah Hotel and planned our sightseeing so he would have adequate rest and receive his injections on schedule. Every five hours he filled the syringe and brought it to me, waking me during the night at the appropriate hour.

Wherever we went, people were attracted to Russell. Many approached him on the street, giving him the very thing he wanted—an opportunity to witness. He shared Christ with everyone he met. After two days in Jerusalem, he suggested we return to Tel Aviv. From there we drove to the beautiful city of Haifa, arriving in late afternoon. The strenuous trip had drained Russell's energy, and he seemed to take a turn for the worse. But after resting through the night and eating green vegetables, he began to regain strength.

On the sixth day, Russell woke me at three in the morning and asked me to give him an injection. Handing me the syringe, he said, "Harold, this is the last of the drugs."

"What?" I asked, stunned.

"I was supposed to take one vial every five hours, but the pain was so bad, I've had to double the dose. "There's no more morphine."

I was frantic. By morning Russell was trembling with pain

again, and he was spitting up parts of the tumor. I went to
see the local druggist. He read the letter from Russell's doctor and said he could not give us the drugs. When I begged
him to call Russell's doctor collect, he refused.

I returned to the hotel to call the doctor myself, and when
I arrived, I could see that Russell was deteriorating rapidly.
When I reached Birmingham on the telephone, the doctor
was in surgery. I left a message with Russell's mother to get
in touch with the doctor.

By late afternoon, Russell was bleeding from the mouth,
spitting up dead tissue, and slipping in and out of conscious-
ness. Desperate, I telephoned several doctors and pleaded
for help, but none of them understood the urgency of our
situation. I thought of robbing the drugstore, then shoved
the thought aside. Desolate, I fell to my knees beside
Russell's bed and prayed.

Reading again the letter from Russell's doctor, I noticed
for the first time a passage of Scripture he had penned on
the top of the page: "Therefore, whether you eat or drink,
or whatever you do, do all to the glory of God"
(1 Corinthians 10:31). The words comforted me.

Moments later the telephone rang. It was the druggist,
who said that Russell's doctor had called. If I could find a
doctor to write a prescription, he would fill it. The druggist gave me the number of a physician who spoke English.
He came to the hotel right away.

After examining Russell, the doctor said, "He's dying. He
may not live through the night. What are you doing in Israel
at a time like this?"

While the doctor gave Russell a series of injections, I
repeated the story. The doctor shook his head in amazement.

"Here is enough medication for the night," he said. "I will
check on him at eight in the morning. If he is alive, I will
see that the druggist gives you all the medication you need."

Through the night I administered Russell's shots and
prayed. About 3 A.M. he opened his eyes. I ran to the bed
and squeezed his hand. He was thirsty and asked for an

orange drink. I hunted the streets of Haifa and finally returned an hour later with the drink. In the morning I bought vegetables for him and bathed him before the doctor arrived. Surprised to find the patient much improved, he went to see the druggist and returned with enough medication for the remainder of our stay in Israel.

After resting for two days, Russell was ready to go again; we headed for the coastal city of Nahariya. Russell phoned a Christian family who had recently moved there from Great Britain, and we were invited to visit. While Russell rested, our hosts' nine-year-old son, David, came to me. His eyes were dark with sorrow.

"Why is he dying? It's not fair!"

"Son, there are many things I don't understand," I said. "God's ways are not our ways, and His thoughts aren't ours. Right now I can't tell you why this is happening, but you must trust God. One day we will understand."

"Will you do me a favor?" he asked. "When you go back to the United States, will you call me if Russell dies?"

"I promise," I said.

When it was time to leave, David's father followed us to the car with a Bible in his hand.

"I'd like to share a verse of Scripture with you before you go," he said. The verse he read was 1 Corinthians 10:31: "Therefore, whether you eat or drink, or whatever you do, do all to the glory of God."

Russell gave me a knowing look and said, "Angels, brother, angels!"

On the way back to Jerusalem we hit a rugged stretch of road going about thirty-five miles per hour. In the middle of nowhere, the car left the road and came to a stop in a rocky area, nearly turning over. Russell was thrown to the floor. I visualized the headline: *Ex-Convict Kills Boy Dying of Cancer in Israel.* The engine had stopped on impact, and I was certain the car had sustained heavy damage. But I turned on the ignition, and to my surprise, the motor started. After backing out of the rocks, I looked the car over. There wasn't a dent, and it ran as well as it had before the accident. Again Russell offered an explanation: "Angels, brother, angels!"

The next day, we attended a worship service at the Garden Tomb, believed to be the setting of Christ's resurrection. I bundled Russell up in a blanket to shield him against the early morning chill. Looking toward Golgotha, the rocky hill where Jesus was crucified, Russell spoke softly. "He's real, Harold. He's alive. Tell others that He is alive."

The following day, we were invited to the home of a girl named Esther, whom we had met at the Garden Tomb. There were about twenty-five guests, and several trusted Christ after Russell gave his testimony. As soon as we returned to our hotel, she telephoned.

"You will not believe this," she said. "But tomorrow you and Russell have been invited to the Knesset to visit Yechiel Kadishai. He is the second most powerful man in the country—Prime Minister Begin's top aide and closest friend!"

How had such an unlikely meeting been arranged? It seems that Esther—an ordinary girl with courage reminiscent of the biblical queen—recognized in Russell such love for Christ that she called Mr. Kadashai. When she explained that Russell had come to Israel because of his great love for the Jewish people, he agreed to meet with us.

Russell stayed awake all night writing two messages from Romans 10 and 11. The next day—Christmas Eve—Esther drove us to the Knesset, where we were welcomed warmly by Mr. Kadishai.

"Come in. I've been expecting you," he said, shaking our hands. As we walked into his office, I noticed a door to the left. Mr. Kadashai pulled a chair close to Russell and sat facing him. Russell unfolded one of the messages he had prepared, opened his Bible, and shared with the Israeli leader about Christ the Messiah.

After a while Mr. Kadishai took the Bible and shared with Russell from the Old Testament. He then presented me with an autographed copy of a book he had written, *Myths and Facts of 1978, a Concise Record of the Arab-Israeli Conflict.*

After I related my story and shared my faith in Christ, Mr. Kadishai spoke.

"So you were in prison?" he said, "Menachem Begin was in solitary confinement in Russia. He wrote a book, *White Nights,* detailing his experiences. Mr. Begin chose the title because the desert nights—viewed from his prison cell— were never dark."

Mr. Kadishai rose and disappeared through the door I had noticed when we entered the room. In a moment he returned with Menachem Begin!

"May God bless, young man," Mr. Begin said as he shook my hand. Then, turning to Russell, his warm expression changed to shock at the severity of Russell's condition. He walked over to Russell and extended his hand in friendship.

"May God be with you, young man," Mr. Begin said.

Without a moment's hesitation, Russell reached into his pocket for his second message and handed it to Israel's Prime Minister.

"Mr. Begin, I prepared this for you. If you'll study it, sir, you'll see that Jesus is the Messiah. One day every knee will bow and every tongue confess that He is Lord."

Mr. Begin placed the paper in his pocket and talked with us for a long while. Finally, I said to Mr. Begin, "Thank you, sir, for letting us come today. It is a day we will never forget. But I must share one thing before we leave. When Russell was told he had perhaps only four days to live, I asked what he wanted to do with his life. He said he wanted to come to Israel, and to die in this country. He loves you and your people enough that he has come here to die." Mr. Begin wrapped his arms around Russell as a father would embrace his son, and I saw tears in his eyes as he spoke.

"May God be with you, young man, because you are a winner. And one day you will return to Israel." He turned and left the room.

Russell and I returned to our hotel, marveling that God had brought such important men into our lives. We spent Christmas Day in Bethlehem, the birthplace of our Savior.

That night we attended a worship service in the field of Boaz. The message, "Mary Had a Little Lamb," rang with meaning. I wrapped my arm around Russell and thought of the life and death of the blessed Lamb of God.

Russell's health continued to decline daily, and he seemed satisfied that he had accomplished what God wanted him to do in Israel. I arranged for an earlier flight home. God had blessed our journey beyond my expectations. Although we had no advanced reservations, He always found a room for us. He protected Russell from diarrhea, which the doctor warned would be deadly in his weakened condition. And He opened numerous opportunities for Russell to share his faith.

Having lived his dream, Russell no longer smiled. On the plane he expended all his energy witnessing. His suffering intensified hour by hour, and although I knew God was in charge, I couldn't understand why He was allowing this. The closer we got to New York, the more distressed I became.

In New York I carried him through the airport like a rag doll and sat him in a chair while I called his mother; he fell asleep. As we arrived in Birmingham at 3 A.M. Russell squeezed my hand weakly and said, "Let's pray." I'll never forget his words:

"Father, thank You for letting me live my dream. Thank you for bringing me home to see my mother once more. And Father, please bless those who are less fortunate than I am." I saw that he was crying, and I knew he was praying for me. Russell faced his death with calm serenity while I was distraught. He thought I was less fortunate because I did not see God's hand in his suffering.

Russell lived forty-two days after our arrival back in the United States and I saw him nearly every day. On the morning of February 7, 1980, Russell had been scheduled to speak at the Georgia State Penitentiary. When he realized he didn't have the strength to make it, he urged me to go in his place.

I called the hospital that morning and spoke with him. "Russell, I love you, and I want to thank you for the impact you've had on my life. I've lived many years, but you are so young. If I could, I would take your place and die with honor."

"I know that," Russell whispered. Struggling for breath, he added, "You're a loyal friend, Harold, but never forget this: it's loyalty to Christ that counts."

That was our last conversation. A few hours later, Russell was with Jesus. Through his friendship, I learned that it isn't the length of one's life that counts, but the quality of one's years. God had received more glory from Russell's twenty-two years than from all the time I had lived.

In prison I had learned that loyalty to friends is good, but from Russell I learned that faithfulness to Christ is far more important. Seeing Russell's faith caused mine to grow.

Accepting his death, I saw what man's existence is all about. Romans 1:16 was the theme of his life: "For I am not ashamed of the gospel of Christ, for it is the power of God to salvation for everyone who believes, for the Jew first and also for the Greek."

That was Russell Moore. His life was woven into the fabric of my being, a continual reminder of what mighty things God can do through the man who is faithful.

CHAPTER 15

TWICE PARDONED

Back at Southeastern Bible College, I plunged into my studies with renewed vigor. As the months passed and I moved closer to graduation, I kept thanking God for all that I was learning. The greatest lessons were gleaned not from a textbook but from precious experience. I learned that we receive from life what we put into it; there are no "free lunches." I learned that we serve a big God, and there is no limit to what He will do when we give Him the glory for our lives.

Nonetheless, my efforts in the classroom were rewarding, and my grades steadily improved as I gained study skills and understanding.

One day I walked into the student union building and found my name on the Dean's List for academic excellence.

"Hey, that's me! Harold Morris!"

"Big deal," said a young freshman.

"Listen, punk," I said merrily, "have you ever known anyone who was on the FBI's Ten Most Wanted List *and* on the Dean's List at Bible college?"

In March 1981—just two months before I was to graduate—I sent a letter to the governor of Georgia and the Pardons and Parole Board requesting a pardon. When I first suggested this to my parole officer, he laughed and insisted that I was expecting the impossible.

"You said you believed in me," I reminded him.

"I really do," he said. "More than any inmate I've ever known, I believe in you."

"Then write a letter for me."

He wrote a one-page letter stating that I would be graduating from Bible college on May 16, 1981, and that I wanted to be free of all travel restrictions in order to better serve Jesus Christ. The letter urged prayerful consideration of my request for a pardon. Weeks passed, but no reply came.

At 10 A.M. on May 15, I finished my last exam, completing a four-year program in three years. As I headed for the student union building to celebrate with my friends, one of the professors stopped to offer congratulations and inquire about my future plans.

"I'm returning to South Carolina to start a full-time ministry," I explained. "I'm going to serve the Lord with my life."

"A few months ago, you asked me to pray about your being pardoned," she remembered. "Have you heard anything?"

"No, but I honestly believe that when I graduate tomorrow, I'll be free to serve Jesus Christ. I'm going to hear," I said. She walked away, shaking her head.

It was about 2 P.M. when I returned to my apartment. An hour later the phone rang.

"Come downtown quickly," my parole officer said.

"Is something wrong?" I asked. "Did somebody rob a bank?" I persisted, only half-joking.

"Hey, smartie, get on down here!"

When I reached his office, he handed me a letter from the Pardon and Parole Board and the governor of Georgia. It said that the crime against me had been erased and my rights as a citizen of the United States had been restored. I was no longer on probation. At last I was truly free to serve Christ.

"This is not from man; it is from God," I said. "Many years ago Jesus Christ gave me a pardon when He forgave my sins and offered me eternal life. Now He has pardoned me a second time!"

The parole officer looked at me through tears and replied, "You know, Harold, you've got me believing in God!"

Good news is always better when it's shared, but no one was around to hear. My college friends were busy with affairs on campus, and many of my out-of-state friends were at that very moment traveling to Birmingham for my graduation. As if on cue, the phone rang. It was a friend, Gene Anderson, from Myrtle Beach, South Carolina, calling to say he would be unable to attend graduation and would be praying for me. When he heard about the miracle pardon, he cried.

At six o'clock I drove to the campus for a candlelight service. The darkened auditorium assumed a warm glow as each senior entered carrying a candle. We were given just thirty seconds to state our name, major, hometown, type of ministry, and other plans or goals. Finally, my turn came to address the students and faculty members. Many of them had prayed with me and for me during the past three years. I recognized many friends who had traveled a great distance to share this occasion—a moment they helped to make a reality through their prayer and financial support.

"I'm afraid I'll need more than thirty seconds!" I began. "Many of you don't know my background. I received Christ in prison, and later God freed me. This school accepted me and educated me, and now I'm graduating to enter full-time ministry. When I applied for a pardon two months ago, many people gave me very little hope. Today I received a letter which I'd like to read to you." As I shared the content of the letter, the auditorium became filled with the sound of rejoicing as Christ was glorified.

The graduation ceremony came on the following day. When I walked across the stage to receive my diploma, I received a standing ovation. (I think everybody was glad to be rid of me!) The honor really belonged to the strength of my life, Christ Jesus. It felt good to accomplish something for the Savior.

Several years later, I met all five members of the Pardon and Parole Board and thanked them personally for believing in me. The chairman—who had told me years earlier that I'd never be released from prison—shook my hand, said he was proud to know me, and asked me to keep in touch. I thanked God that those men and the governor had the courage to set me free!

The last thing an ex-convict wants to do is go back to prison! Nevertheless, on May 21, 1978, I returned to Georgia State Penitentiary—not as an inmate but as a minister of the gospel of Jesus Christ. The warden had granted permission for me to lead a service, and Bobby Richardson was to speak. I had written to several inmates that I was coming. As I walked in the door, an officer threw his arms around me.

"Man, I miss you!" he said. It was the guard I'd threatened to assign to tower six! He turned to Bobby and said, "There's never been another inmate like Harold Morris. He's one of the finest men I've ever met. He saved my job! I love him!"

Another guard said, "When I go to your old cell, the guys there now won't even speak to me. They look at me like I'm an animal. You used to talk to me. I really miss you." These comments from prison officers meant a great deal to me as I remembered the bad attitude I'd had when I first came to the prison. Again I was aware of God's infinite power to change people.

A black inmate—a con artist who had spent most of his sixty-plus years in prison serving numerous short sentences—said, "Mr. Richardson, I want to tell you about Super Honky. The Honky don't know this, but he led me to the Lord. The Honky's the best white athlete who ever come to this prison. He was different, and I wondered what it was. One day I asked him. He say, 'You need Jesus in your life.' I go up to my cell and I think about that. I give my heart to Jesus. I miss ol' Super Honky. He's different from all the rest. He's the only one come back to see us."

Since my release I've been to Georgia State Penitentiary more than fifty times. For one crusade, Betsy Richardson (Bobby's wife) and her friends baked seventy cakes for the inmates. The men were overwhelmed with such a delicious gesture of friendship.

In prisons throughout the country, I have spoken to as many as a thousand inmates on the prison football field. But I prefer witnessing in individual cells. The large meetings and chapel services merely break the ice for personal evangelism. I usually spend the day, going from cell to cell, including those on death row. It's a hard way to witness, but it's very effective. The masses are interested in what I can do for them; they try to con me by asking for material things. But sharing one-on-one, I get inside a man. When he opens his heart to me, Jesus really has a chance to work.

As a young Christian in prison, I realized the greatest need in my life was discipleship. That has become the thrust of my ministry—discipling those who are serious in their commitment, those who want to learn more about Jesus Christ and His Word. God has given me discernment to separate genuine believers from phonies. I don't hesitate to be firm with the men. Immediately I level with an inmate who tries to con me. When I find one who really wants to study the Word and grow in Christ, I disciple him. An inmate who is excited about Jesus can win more people to Christ behind bars than most people ever could on the outside.

However, sometimes the people who most need help are those you least want to befriend. For example, I was reluctant to become involved in the life of an inmate named Matt. Matt was not my kind of person. He was serving two life sentences after being convicted of raping two women. We spent almost ten years together in prison, but I avoided him, even after becoming a Christian.

His was a tragic story. As a boy of ten—after being physically abused by his adoptive parents—he killed his mother with a baseball bat. Neighbors raised money to fight the murder charge, and he was freed. But his recent crimes put him back behind bars.

Shortly before parole I began spending time with Matt. On my last night in prison, I had visited him and told him I loved him and was coming back to help him.

His response was predictable. "Yeah, they all say that."

I did go back, each time inviting Matt to the chapel service. He refused to come. On my eighth visit to the pentitentiary, I noticed Matt leaning against the wall in the chapel. I motioned for him to sit with me. Again I told him I loved him, but he made no reply. A short time later, I felt a nudge on my shoulder and turned around. It was Matt.

"You really care, don't you?" he said. "I know you hated prison as much as anybody who's ever been here, but you've come back eight times."

"Yes I do care. I love you."

A friend of mine preached that night, and when he gave the invitation to come to Christ, I felt another nudge.

Matt was crying. "Would you help me?" he said. "I want to trust Christ."

After sharing several Scriptures with him from Romans, I knelt with him to pray. After I started the prayer, Matt finished, giving his heart to Jesus. I knew he was saved when he stopped *asking* Jesus to save him and started *thanking* Jesus for saving him!

He stood at the front of the chapel and told the other inmates he had given his heart to Christ and that he wanted to change. He became involved in Bible study and began to grow in the Lord. Shortly thereafter he invited me to speak to the Lifer's Club, composed of inmates who had served at least five years of a life sentence and have been model prisoners. The group made me an honorary member. After I finished speaking, Matt asked for a few minutes on the program.

Pulling a newspaper clipping from his pocket, he showed the picture of a five-year-old boy who had been attacked by a bulldog. The child's family did not have the financial means to cover surgical costs.

"This little boy's face will be disfigured for the rest of his life unless he has surgery," he said. "I'm taking up money to help pay his medical expenses." I realized that Matt could relate to the youngster because his own face was somewhat disfigured.

"Some of you have made fun of me," he said. "I can handle it because I'm a man. But this little boy deserves a chance."

We all contributed that night. Some gave cash, others gave cigarettes, and a few gave watches. The collection totaled nearly $700. The local newspaper heard about the inmate with a generous heart and carried a story about his fund-raising efforts, along with a picture of Matt, the child, and father. I realized two things: Matt had a heart that the whole world needed, and he deserved to be out of prison. God gave me a burden to fight for his freedom. I made him a promise.

"One day you'll be a free man. I believe in you."

I went before the parole board with several of my Christian friends to plead his case. A year later, in March 1980, after spending twelve years in prison, Matt was paroled.

I'll never forget the day I picked him up at the prison. As we walked out, both of us were crying. Looking up at the familiar guard tower, I said, "It's a great day! The sun is shining. It's a new beginning. It's the start of your new life. We were told we would die here, but today we're free! No dogs are barking, and no shotguns are firing at us. We're free! He's a big God, isn't He?"

With guards and others watching, we bowed on our knees in the parking lot to thank Jesus for life and freedom.

A fine Christian man in South Carolina—a member of my board of directors—and his wife took Matt in, gave him a job, settled him into a church, and discipled him. During the years since his release, he has been true to the Lord. He taught me, as have so many others, that when the Spirit of God enters a man's heart, that person becomes a new creature. He has hope and a purpose in life.

That same lesson was taught me by Mike Godwin, who was on death row at the state penitentiary in Columbia, South Carolina. There he had earned a reputation of being the most violent man in the prison. He was sentenced to die in the electric chair after a jury declared him guilty of rape and murder.

Spending six months as a death-row inmate was the most horrible experience of my years in prison, yet I thank God for it. I learned how condemned men think. I felt their fears. Because I understand them, I can communicate with them. I've witnessed on death row in five states.

On one of these trips I visited the prison where Mike Godwin was awaiting execution. When I arrived, I was told the twenty-one-year-old inmate had almost killed a guard and another inmate in a fight the previous day. The other death-row inmates were brought to a small room where I shared for a couple of hours. Afterward, the warden asked me to visit Mike, who was being punished in a detention cell that resembled a dungeon.

"We don't know what to do with him," the warden said. "Would you witness to him?"

Oh, man, would I!

He led me to a room with concrete walls and a metal door. The inmate walked in wearing handcuffs to prevent him from hurting me.

"What do you want?" he growled. "It's none of the religion junk, is it?"

"No, no, I promise." That was really all I knew to share, but I walked over to him and shook his hand.

"I'm sorry about your handcuffs. I wish they'd take them off," I said.

"What do you want?" he repeated.

"They tell me you're violent, that you almost killed a guard and an inmate yesterday."

"That's right," he replied.

"They tell me you're the most violent man here."

"That's right," he said impatiently.

"I don't think you're violent; I think you're angry," I surmised.

"That's it!" he exclaimed "I'm not violent; I'm angry."

I breathed a sigh of relief.

"Mike, I know you don't want to hear any religion junk, and I'm not going to tell you any religion junk. But I want

to tell you about Jesus Christ and what He means in my life.
You see, I spent nine-and-a-half years in prison."

"You?"

"Yes." I shared with him about my prison days and the
friends who gave me a Bible and Scripture verses that led
me to Christ. I told him of my Christian growth during those
final five years in prison and stressed that Jesus is real. I
talked for about an hour.

Mike looked at me with tears in his eyes and said, "I don't
want to trust any Christ. I don't believe in God. But would
you pray with me?"

"You bet I will!"

I prayed for God to make His power known to this angry
young man.

"Mike, I must leave, but I'll be back."

"Yeah, they all say that."

"I'll be back," I said again.

I went back every week for a while. Although I didn't see
Mike, he knew I had come as promised. When I shared with
death-row inmates again in June 1982, Mike was out of detention. He hugged me and stood near me as I spoke to the
group for about forty-five minutes. When I finished, I felt a
nudge on my shoulder. Again there were tears in Mike's
eyes.

"Will you help me?" he said. "I don't ever want to hurt
anybody again."

"Of course, I will," I said, and then opened my Bible.
"Mike, it's obvious that you have an extremely high I.Q. I
want you to write this down." He began to write as I shared:

"Romans 3:10, 'As it is written: *There is none righteous,
no not one.*'"

"Romans 3:23, 'For *all* have sinned and fall short of the
glory of God.'"

"Romans 6:23, 'For the wages of sin is death, but the gift
of God is eternal life in Christ Jesus our Lord.'"

"Mike, that same God loves you because of Romans 5:8,"
I explained. "But God demonstrates His own love toward

us, in that while we were still sinners, Christ died for us.'"

"Let me see that," he said.

I showed him that truth clearly stated in black and white in God's Word, and then moved on to Romans 10:13: "'For *whoever* calls upon the name of the Lord shall be saved.'"

"That's you, me, or anyone who calls upon His name," I pointed out. I turned to Romans 10:9. "'That if you confess with your mouth the Lord Jesus and believe in your heart that God has raised Him from the dead, you will be saved.'"

"Mike, don't take my word for it," I said. "Don't trust me. I love you, but I'll fail you—not because I want to but because I'm human. However, Jesus will never fail you. You're intelligent. I want you to go to your cell and read these Scriptures. Give God a chance to speak to your heart, and you'll respond." I gave him a Bible. Two days later I received a letter from Mike.

"After you left I went to my death-row cell, opened that Bible, and read the Scriptures you gave me—every word over and over. For the first time in my life, I realized the truth. I got on my knees and gave my heart to Jesus Christ. I'd rather be here and be the man I am today than be on the streets free. Would you help me grow?"

I could hardly wait to go back to the prison. Mike was a changed man, eager to learn of Christ and lead others to Him. Like a starving man, he devoured the Bible studies I brought. He enrolled in correspondence study at Columbia Bible College and later added courses from the University of South Carolina. In August 1985, he completed requirements for a two-year associate degree at the University of South Carolina, and in June 1986, he received a Bachelor of Arts degree with a 3.85 grade point average. God is using him in a tremendous way inside prison as well as outside through letters to young people.

I have encouraged teenagers across the country to write to Mike about their problems. A girl in Arkansas told him of her plans to drop out of school and run away from home. Complaining of a poor relationship with her parents and conflict with her boyfriend, she said everything was falling apart, and she couldn't take it anymore.

Mike not only answered her letters but also made cassette tapes for her. However, the girl rejected his advice and decided to go through with her plan. It was time to be firm.

"Go ahead and leave," Mike wrote. "But don't write to me again if you aren't going to do as I say. I don't have time to play. You need to get on your knees before God and then go to your mother and daddy to ask forgiveness. You need to take advantage of that school and the discipline it offers. You need to thank God for those teachers. Go ahead and leave home, but I'll tell you what will happen. You'll turn to drugs and end up pregnant."

Surprisingly, the girl did not rebel against his rebuke. Not long afterwards, she wrote to me.

"Because of Mike and you, I went home to my family and asked their forgiveness. I gave my heart to Jesus Christ. I graduated from school. By the way, I was valedictorian. I'm going to have the best life of all! Thank God for both of you."

God gave me a burden to fight for Mike's life, and I raised $5,000 to cover legal fees for a new trial. He was given a life sentence and moved to another prison, where he has more freedom. I feel the peace of the Lord that someday he will be free.

I don't help every inmate. Before I try to obtain freedom for someone, I must believe the man is a born-again Christian who will commit himself to study the Word of God over a period of time. I must believe he can function in society. And I must feel led of the Lord to do it. God is the one who opens the door, even as He did for me. It's in His hands.

Jesus hates murder, but He loves the murderer. I go to prisons—my Judea—to tell men about the love of Christ which covers all sin. I have spoken to more than a million people—sometimes to a crowd of 50,000 and sometimes to one.

One time in a federal prison in Memphis, Tennessee, I had just started to speak when the chapel service was interrupted. An inmate who looked vaguely familiar rose from his seat on the front row and faced the crowd. I didn't know what he planned to do.

"What this man is about to say is true," he announced to his fellow inmates. "I did six years with him at Georgia State Penitentiary. He was one of the meanest and toughest men there. If Jesus Christ can save him, He can save any of us."

A holy hush fell over the chapel, and revival resulted. There were many decisions for Christ. After the service I talked briefly with the inmate and learned that he had been at the Tennessee facility for several years after getting into trouble following his release from the penitentiary. That night he renewed his commitment to Christ.

Again and again I have heard the stories of repeat offenders like that inmate. Although the very word *penitentiary* implies repentence and reformation, I'm concerned that the prison system has not been successful at rehabilitating inmates.

I remember a nineteen-year-old inmate who came to Georgia State Penitentiary with a three-year sentence for stealing an automobile. He was literally scared to death. But after a short time, some old cons took him in and made a drug runner out of him. After spending a year in prison, he became a tough guy, ready to pursue a life of crime. When paroled, he took to the streets.

Prison doesn't *teach* a man to commit crimes, but it gives him the *will* to become more criminally active. That happened to the boy. Before he left the prison, one of the old cons gave him an Atlanta address. In that home was a safe full of money, he said. "Rob it and you'll be fixed for life."

The kid took a bus to Atlanta, located the house, and knocked. A fifteen-year-old girl opened the door. No one knows what was said, but he killed the girl and her mother. There was no money in the safe. Sentenced to die in the electric chair, the boy now waits on death row. For ten years he has waited. When I visited his cell, I asked, "How are you doing?"

"I'm through, Harold. I'm through," he said, ashamed to look at me.

Sadly enough, he *is* through. He came to prison as an innocent youngster who stole an automobile for a joyride. He left with a chip on his shoulder, determined to get even with the system. There are a million stories like this.

All prisons are full of losers—people who wanted something for nothing, who followed the wrong crowd, who rejected discipline, who refused to work, who never learned to manage their lives. And yet *I* was once a loser. *I* once wanted something for nothing. *I* once followed the crowd. Even so, because God loved me and because Christians chose to live out the Incarnation in my life, I *was* rehabilitated—and twice pardoned!

CHAPTER 16

MY JERUSALEM

Abundantly above all that I could ask or think, God has honored the commitment that I voiced as I left Georgia State Penitentiary—to make young people my Jerusalem. In high schools throughout America, I've found that young people are hungrier and more desperate to hear the Word of God than adults are to share it with them. They live in a different age than I knew growing up, and they face pressures which I never faced. But God has given me the ability to relate to young people. They know I love them, and they do not feel threatened. They open their hearts to me.

During the past six years I have spoken in more than 500 high schools and junior high schools. I discuss alcohol and drugs, negative peer pressure and how to resist it, self-esteem, and wrong associations and what they can do to one's life. I stress the importance of developing a good attitude, accepting discipline at home and at school, loving and understanding one's parents. I let young people know that I love them and that Jesus died for them. I warn them of the danger of making even a little compromise, such as cheating on a test or smoking cigarettes.

Following one high school assembly program, a teenager handed a pack of cigarettes to me.

"My dad would kill me if he knew I smoked cigarettes and drank beer," he said. "What you told us is true. First it's cigarettes, then marijuana, next it's beer, and finally sex. Everything you said has happened to me. I want you to know

I'm through with that dead-end lifestyle. Thank you, sir. I wish I could have met you a long time ago."

"It's never too late," I told him. "You've learned a lesson. Now you can help your friends. Your whole life is ahead of you. I'm so proud of you!"

Another boy gave me a handful of marijuana leaves used to wrap joints.

"I'm through with this stuff," he said.

"Where's the marijuana?" I asked.

"In the car."

"Get it. I won't turn you in," I promised.

Minutes later he returned with the marijuana.

"Now I believe in you," I said. "If you hadn't gone after the marijuana, your words wouldn't have meant much."

"I'm through," he repeated. "Thank you, sir."

Before speaking in a school, I always ask the principal if I'm allowed to share about Jesus Christ. I don't want to abuse the privilege that I've been given. Many times I am free to present the gospel, and often the students give me an opportunity by asking about my commitment to Christ.

One day I was in a large high school in Georgia with Roy Carter, state director of the Fellowship of Christian Athletes. After getting acquainted with the principal, I asked the usual questions.

"How much time do I have?"

"As much as you want," the principal said.

"Sir, am I allowed to speak the name of Jesus here?" I asked.

"I'd sure hope so," he said.

"Some schools won't allow me," I said.

"We haven't been asked to prohibit it here."

"May I pray and give an invitation?"

"If you don't, I will," he declared.

The gym was packed with kids. I stood in center court and spoke for an hour and twenty minutes, closing with a challenge.

"Some of you will raise your finger at the ball game and

shout, 'We're number one!' Are there any men and women here today who will stand with me and make Jesus Christ number one in your life?"

So many youths came forward that the principal instructed the students to meet in a classroom if they wished to talk with me further. Seeing that the room would not accommodate the crowd, the principal announced on the public address system that all who were interested could meet me on the football field. The entire student body came. I stood at the fifty-yard line for an additional hour sharing and answering many questions. When I finally had to leave for another speaking engagement, the students gave Jesus a standing ovation. If more schools had warriors like that principal, we'd see different kids.

When speaking to students, I demand respect and I give it. If the kids are noisy and inattentive, I grab the microphone and say firmly, "Let me tell you something. You shut your mouth or I'll run you out of here." The gym grows quiet, and they can hear me say, "I love you, and I'm sorry I have to speak firmly. Thank you for listening." Invariably, the students who were out of order apologize later. Students need discipline, and I'm convinced they want it.

With black students I have an especially good rapport because they know my background. They realize I spent two-and-a-half years in a cell with a black inmate, who became one of my closest friends. They know I understand them because I was once an underdog, too.

Thousands of young people have written to me. After speaking to more than 1,000 youths in an Arkansas school, I returned to my home in Myrtle Beach, South Carolina. A few days later a letter arrived from a seventeen-year-old high school senior.

"I would give anything to have heard your story years ago," she said. "I use drugs, I drink alcohol, and I'm pregnant. I have to drop out of school. My mother has rejected me. I want to die!"

I wrote immediately, advising her to go to a church for

help. Her next letter brought sad news. The church had turned her away. In prison I saw inmates die for men they hardly knew. It's a tragedy that Christians have earned a reputation for shooting the wounded.

In my letters I encouraged the girl to seek the Lord and His strength. Her mother, after recovering from the initial shock, became supportive. And when the baby was born, the girl sent a joyful letter.

"He's the prettiest baby! I love him and I'm going to bring him up to be a godly boy."

When I returned to Arkansas a year later, I drove forty miles to visit the young woman. She had finished high school and found a church where she was accepted. Because she followed God's wisdom, she has a productive life helping young people with problems similar to hers.

Another teenager wrote a year after hearing me speak. She was a member of a punk rock band, and she was involved with drugs and sexual immorality. Convinced that she had no reason to live, she wanted to kill herself. She couldn't explain why she had come to the service that night, but she gave her heart to Christ. The rest of the story is a testimony to God's life-transforming power. She enrolled in Bible college, where she made the Dean's List. She married a young Christian man and together they are serving the Lord.

Thank God for the young people whose paths have crossed mine! At a crusade one night, a teenager told me she was planning to commit suicide. She said her father had raped her, and although he no longer lived with the family, she still suffered from this grievous emotional wound. I gave her my phone number and asked her to call me so that we could talk further. She did call and also began writing. Her letters were filled with hopelessness.

"I am writing this letter four days after my graduation," she said, "and I feel terrible. I have so much pain and hurt eating at me inside that I am about to explode. You know, I still wish I were dead, but I haven't got the nerve to do it—not yet anyway. I just feel so empty and alone. I'm not happy with myself. I feel so cheap inside about my past.

Even though it happened four years ago, the scars are still there. I've tried to put it aside, but something always brings it back. You know, I'm just downright tired of everything . . . .

"Sometimes I wish I had a father who was different. I don't want my real father; I could never love him again. I have forgiven him for what he did to me, but that doesn't change what happened. I can never love him, and I wouldn't let myself even if I wanted to. I just wish I had an adopted father, someone who cares and won't reject me . . . .

"I'm so alone. People tell me to give all to Jesus, but it doesn't work. I'm saved, but still I'm so confused about everything.

"I hope I haven't bored you. Most people who supposedly care really don't . . . How many times I've come to the point of just wanting to die! . . . Someone is always better than I am. I feel so rejected at times that if I just blew my head off, very few (I mean *very* few) people would notice . . . . I'm fighting a losing battle. You know, it's pretty lonely . . . . "

Could anything make a difference in the life of this desperate teenager? I had to find out. I asked her to tell me something she would really like to do. She wanted to attend a Christian camp, so I arranged to sponsor her. With that experience her life began to change. She started singing in church and seemed hopeful for the first time since we had met.

I asked if she planned to attend college. She could not afford it for a while, she said, but she wanted to study to become a paramedic. So I sent her to paramedic school, and she later graduated. Today this young woman who wanted to die is a vibrant twenty-year-old with a job in a hospital, a steady boyfriend, a strong faith in God, and a bright outlook for the future. Believing in herself and developing her potential made a difference in her life. She still phones me several times a month, and I visit her when I'm in the area.

A thirteen-year-old seventh grader approached me after I finished speaking at her school.

"Could I talk to you before you leave?" she said. She was one of the most beautiful girls I had ever seen. "What you said really meant a lot to me and my friends," she began. "One of my friends is thinking about taking her life."

"Honey, go get her," I urged. "I've got to talk to her before I leave."

"I can't," she said.

"Please! I must see her."

She hesitated, and then quietly said, "You're talking to her."

"You? You're so beautiful! Why would you ever think about such a thing?"

"Nobody understands," she said. "Nobody listens to me. My parents give me everything I want. We're wealthy, but I don't need anything—except love."

I was so glad to share the Good News with her!

"There are at least two people who love you. I love you and Jesus loves you. Your whole life is ahead of you. You can be anything you want to be. These are important years of your life. You've got to make something of them. You have every reason in the world to live. Promise me you'll call before you try to take your life!" Her letters indicate that she is doing well, but her story wrenched my heart.

Love! The missing ingredient in so many homes today! And the parents aren't even aware. Many a father has said to me, "I work hard to make a living. Somebody has to pay the bills. I do everything for my kid. He's thinking about suicide? I can't believe this! Our home has love!"

These parents do their best to share love, but kids see love differently. A new bicycle or a new automobile is not love in the kid's eyes. Giving a hug or a kiss, going to a ballgame or the zoo—in these, a kid sees love.

If a teenager is prepared to stand on his own in a sick, hurting, dying world, it will be because parents have taken time to deal with his problems—taken time, that is, to love!

Young people want something real. They're tired of the double standard: a parent with a beer in one hand and a cigarette in the other, preaching, "Do as I say, not as I do." They're looking for role models to serve as a pattern for their lives.

I thank God for giving me a burden for young people and the wisdom to deal with their problems. I know they mean it when they threaten suicide. I know they can take their lives, even though they really don't want to. Don't tell me a person must be insane. I once shared that feeling of desperation. There's not a doubt in my mind that I would have fulfilled my intention to commit suicide if I had obtained the poison. I know the feeling of those who want to die, and that has helped me witness to kids.

Young people know they can share with me because I can keep a confidence. They know I will do what I say because my word is my bond. When I tell them I'll write, I write. When I tell them I'll come back, I do. When I give them my card and ask them to call collect, I'm there when the phone rings. That's what they want—someone to understand them, someone to love and accept them as they are, someone to say, "There's hope, and that hope is the person of Jesus Christ."

CHAPTER 17

ENCOUNTER
WITH A KILLER

Of all the killers I met in prison, I was totally unprepared for the one I encountered during 1984.

In February of that year I noticed a swelling on the left side of my neck, similar to that caused by a bee sting. A fever and sore throat had plagued me for six months, but a physician diagnosed the problem simply as a virus, which improved with medication.

The swelling lasted just a few days, but it left a small knot, and the fever and sore throat recurred. I saw physicians in South Carolina, Ohio, and Colorado as I continued my speaking schedule. After each exam I was given medication and assured there was no reason for concern as the knot did not appear to be symptomatic of any serious disease.

Returning to Atlanta, where I was living, I consulted a physician and underwent another thorough exam. He also believed the knot to be insignificant but advised me to have it removed. The surgeon whom he recommended agreed. The surgery would require only one day of hospitalization and about three days of recovery at home. Since the problem appeared to be minor, I told only a few close friends.

On a Monday in April 1984, at 9 A.M., I entered North Fulton Medical Center in Atlanta. When I awakened from surgery around 3 P.M., the room was very dark, and I was terribly hazy from the anesthesia.

"Can you hear me?" the surgeon asked.

I nodded. He began to talk, but what was he saying? *Bad news. Cancer. Three lymph nodes.* Did he have permission to talk with my friends who were there?

"Yes, tell them anything," I said, sinking into a deep sleep.

When I awakened two hours later, my friends were crying. The doctor was there again. He explained that three lymph nodes on the left side of my neck were malignant, but he didn't know the extent of the cancer. Biopsies were ordered of suspicious tissue. These tests along with numerous others confirmed malignancy behind the left ear, sinuses, and tongue, as well as in my throat. Physicians agreed that with treatment, I might live three years.

After giving my doctors a brief summary of my life, I declared, "Jesus Christ didn't bring me out of prison to let me die of cancer. I'll outlive you!"

I left the hospital on Saturday, and for the first time I was alone. The trauma finally hit with full force. As I lay in bed fighting the pain and the effects of medication, I could see outside the brilliant sun and the trees blowing in the wind. It was a beautiful day, but a feeling of dread draped my being. If the doctors were correct, this was the beginning of a long, hard road for me.

A cancer specialist at Crawford Long Hospital recommended two months of radiation therapy, but he didn't paint a hopeful picture.

"You need a lot of luck and prayer," he said.

It was the most depressing day of my life. How could a tiny lump change things so drastically? Alone in my apartment that night, I tried to sort out the puzzle.

Lord, I don't understand why this is happening, when everything was going so well. For six-and-a-half years I've worked in the ministry to be where I am today. Lord, you've given me an opportunity to witness nationwide through television and radio. My speaking schedule is booked for a year and a half in advance. Lord, the doors are open. This is what I've worked for. Why now?

*Father, I don't want to die. I want to live! I don't understand
this, but You do. Your ways are not our ways, and Your
thoughts are not our thoughts. I want Your will in my life. If
it's Your will I die, I accept that. I know You're trying to
teach me something, and I'll work hard to learn. When I start
the treatment tomorrow, I'll be a good student and a good
patient. I know You work through doctors and medicine. I
won't give up. You've brought me too far. I'm going to fight
this thing, Lord, but it's in Your hands.*

The cancer specialist had referred me to an outstanding
oncologist at St. Joseph's Hospital. After looking over the
medical reports, he pointed out that the primary tumor had
not been found, although it was believed to be in the head
area. He explained that radiation fights cancer cells by blast-
ing them with high-energy rays. Unable to repair the re-
sulting damage or to reproduce themselves, the malignant
cells die. While this sometimes leads to immediate shrinkage
of the tumor or relief from symptoms, he said, often results
are not evident until weeks or months after the treatment
has been completed.

Radiation would be aimed at several areas of the head in
an attempt to destroy the hidden primary tumor, along with
the cancer tissue that had been found. My face and neck
would be painted with a solution to mark the target areas.
Treatment was scheduled for 10:15 A.M. Monday through
Friday for the next eight weeks.

"We're going to fight this thing," the doctor said, although
he gave me only a 32 percent chance for recovery. The odds
were against me, but I knew God was with me.

"Let's go for it!" I agreed.

My face and neck were painted with colorful crosses and
other markings, which would remain throughout the treatment period.

Stopping by a hotel to make reservations for friends, I
realized the clerk was self-conscious, trying not to stare.

"Ma'am, are you wondering what's wrong with me?" I
said.

"Yes. Please tell me, are you a clown?"

"That's right. I'm an entertainer, and I'm looking for work." After leading her on for a short time, I explained I had cancer.

"I'm so sorry!" she said.

"Please don't be sorry," I said. "The death rate is one apiece. We all die. Every day brings each of us closer to death. I might die of cancer, or perhaps be crushed by a car as I leave here."

As a few people gathered around me in the hotel lobby, I began to share my faith in God, the truths He was teaching me, and my excitement that He was going to heal me.

"Just think," I began. "If He doesn't heal me, I'll be in heaven! I'll spend eternity with Him! Isn't that exciting?"

No one seemed excited.

"I've never met anyone like you," the clerk said. "I can't believe your attitude. You handle your illness so well."

"It's because of Christ in me," I stressed.

Following the first radiation treatments, I looked like a lobster. My skin turned pink and darkened. Then it peeled.

After each treatment, I drove the eleven miles from the hospital to my apartment and went to bed. The radiation burned calories, draining my energy; daily I grew weaker. My throat was swollen and unbearably sore. Swallowing became so painful I could no longer eat. Through a straw I sipped water and special liquid nutrients which provided barely enough energy to keep me going.

That period was the most difficult of my life. It was an agonizing, lonely time, yet I was never alone. Always there was God standing with me, and His comforting Holy Spirit encouraging me. He also provided me with very special friends—people whose love was displayed when they cleaned my apartment, drove me to the hospital, and ran errands. Roy Williams, a friend since our days at Guilford College, and his wife, Julia, came from Raleigh, North Carolina. Jim Ryan of the Denver Broncos and his bride, Sarah, spent several days of their honeymoon with me. Another member

of the Broncos, Randy Gradishar, and his wife, Janet, stayed
for two weeks. Many came, and I don't know what I would
have done without them.

Several times at the point of collapse, I was rushed to the
hospital to receive intravenous feeding before the radiation
could continue. At times the pain was so acute I thought I
was dying. There were days when death would have been a
relief. The nurses, so kind and caring, shared my hurt. When
I flinched at having tape removed from around my IV, they
understood my pain.

Shortly before my encounter with cancer, I had completed
a series of cassette tapes dealing with teenage problems, and
I gave a set to several nurses. One came to my room.

"Mr. Morris," she said, "yesterday I listened to the tape
of your testimony while driving to the beauty parlor. I cried
until my mascara ran, and I couldn't go inside to have my
hair done. I just love you!"

Thank God! He hadn't taken me out of the ministry. He
just gave me a different ministry—to doctors, nurses, and
radiation technicians.

The lonely years in prison—particularly the time in solitary confinement—helped me to accept the discipline of
being confined to an apartment for five months. However,
I was not prepared for the emotional trauma of the physical
anguish.

The radiation destroyed good cells along with the cancer
cells. My taste buds were damaged as well as my saliva
glands, but these were expected to return. Other side effects
were diarrhea and vomiting. Through the night my body
racked with dry heaves. Every ten minutes phlegm had to
be cleared from my throat.

A blood sample was taken each Tuesday to determine if
the cancer had spread. My weight dropped steadily—twenty
pounds in matter of days, eighty-five pounds in five months.
Being overweight, I had the pounds to spare, yet before long
I felt like a skeleton.

The hospital waiting room proved to be a most depressing place. Most radiation patients became accustomed to seeing each other. And when someone didn't show up, the news was always the same. "He died last night."

A 26-year-old woman came in, holding a toddler by the hand with another baby in a stroller. When her turn came for treatment she brought the children with her. She never smiled. One day I told her I loved her. She thanked me, but there was not a hint of happiness in her face.

"You seem so depressed," I said.

"How can I not be depressed?" she asked. I told her of my faith in God.

"It's hard to believe in a God who might take me away from my babies," she said.

Silently I prayed, "Please, Lord, give her cancer to me! I already have cancer, and I can handle it. But please don't take her away from those kids!"

During the darkest days of my life, God ministered to my heart through Scripture. The four verses He had used to bring me to himself were very special—1 John 1:9, Romans 6:23, 1 Peter 2:24, and Revelation 3:20. Other verses that gave great comfort were James 1:2–3: "My brethren, count it all joy when you fall into various trials, knowing that the testing of your faith produces patience." Verse 12 also encouraged me: "Blessed is the man who endures temptation; for when he has been proved, he will receive the crown of life which the Lord has promised to those who love Him."

Romans 1:16, the verse Russell Moore had loved, became my favorite as well: "For I am not ashamed of the gospel of Christ, for it is the power of God to salvation for everyone who believes, for the Jew first and also for the Greek."

Many times I was too sick to read God's precious Word, but the Holy Spirit brought to my memory verses that were stored in my heart. What a comfort they were! Many times uncertainty about the future left me with a feeling of confusion, and I searched the Scriptures for peace. One day my

eyes fell on Psalm 118:17–18. Those were the words from
the Lord I'd been waiting for.

> I shall not die, but live,
> And declare the works of the Lord.
> The Lord has chastened me severely,
> But He has not given me over to death.

I claimed those verses, and God used them in a tremendous way. They renewed my hope and determination to fight
for my life.

The final seven treatments were shot directly into my
mouth, turning into one giant blister. I was unable to speak,
and the pain was unbearable. Wet cloths cooled my neck
and face for only a moment before absorbing the intense
body heat.

In my apartment one day, I fainted. Rousing from the
blackness, I crawled to the bedroom and into bed. My heart
pounded, and perspiration drenched the sheets. I crept to
the bathroom for a wet cloth to cool my fiery face, and then
inched my way back to bed. I knew I was going to die. And
in that moment, my lips trembled with prayer:

> *Father, I love You! Thank You for saving me. Lord, I ask not
> that my will be done, but Yours. If it's Your will that I die,
> Lord, I want You to take me home. I want to be with You.
> But I don't want to die. I want to see my mother, my family,
> my friends. Please, Lord! But if death is Your will, I accept
> that.*

After about fifteen minutes, my pounding heart slowed.
God had sent the Angel of Death away.

The treatments were completed close to schedule, and I
returned to the cancer specialist to learn if the radiation had
been effective. If it had not, there was little hope. Because
of the location of the cancer, surgery was not an option, and
further radiation treatments would not even be considered.
After completing the exam, the doctor sat down in a chair
and looked at me.

"This is a miracle," he said. "There is not a trace of cancer. It's the most amazing thing I've ever seen. I can't believe it."

I *could* believe it. I had expected it. However, the radiation damage to my throat would require months of healing. The physician expected me to be eating soft foods very soon. I didn't attempt anything but liquids for several more days, and by the end of the week, my throat had closed completely. I couldn't even swallow water. Suddenly the miracle began to tarnish.

The muscles had contracted from lack of use, and scar tissue had filled the opening. The dilation procedure was very painful, requiring general anesthesia. A rubber tube two-and-a-half feet long had to be inserted regularly for several weeks in an attempt to stretch the opening to forty-eight millimeters—the size of a normal throat. But each time my throat closed again. Finally the physician prepared me for the worst.

"We might have to insert a tube in your throat to feed you for the rest of your life."

"Doctor, you can't say that," I said. "You gave me hope! I'd rather die than have this happen!"

He mentioned the possibility of surgery to rebuild my throat, using tissue from the colon. But after further consideration, he felt this would not be successful because of the amount of scar tissue. One alternative remained: stretching my throat daily myself. The first attempt was so painful it took one hour to insert the two-and-a-half-foot tube. But I eventually became so proficient that I could insert it twice in seven seconds. Surely that was a Guinness record! If anyone challenged me, I was prepared to better my time!

After being warned that I likely would lose my teeth as a result of the radiation, I resorted to the daily gum massaging that had worked so well in prison. Again my teeth were saved!

My taste buds returned gradually, but doctors said my saliva glands would probably never function again. I was forced to sip water constantly to alleviate the leather-like dryness in my throat . . . but I could live with that. One might say that when I spoke, it was an instant message—I just added water!

The cancer went into remission. All visible cancer cells were killed, but the doctors have advised me that the malignancy could recur, especially since the source was never found. While I lived with the reality that it may return, I didn't awake each morning and search for swelling or knots. I just thanked God for the day and lived it to the fullest. Every day was Christmas!

Continually, I praised the Lord for the friends who shared the suffering by praying and supporting me financially. Shortly before the cancer ordeal began, I was interviewed by Ben Kinchlow on *The 700 Club.* God used that program, along with *Focus on the Family,* to enlist prayer support.

Additional help was received from the "grass roots" level. For example, Wes Durham, a student at Apex High School (where I had recorded a tape for Dr. James Dobson's program *Focus on the Family*), suggested that a benefit basketball game be staged to raise money for my medical expenses. The game, promoted by Apex coach John Griggs, was played at Apex High, with former players from North Carolina State competing against former players from University of North Carolina. Several athletes played for professional teams, but they refused to accept even token monetary gifts for participating in the benefit game, which raised $2,000.

As the publicity of my plight spread, thousands of letters poured in from across the country. One that particularly ministered to my heart had been written as though it were from Jesus.

"Harold, I love you. I shed my own blood for you to make you clean. You are new, so believe it is true. You are lovely in my eyes, and I created you to be just as you are. Do not criticize yourself or get down for not being perfect in your own eyes. This leads only to frustration. I want you to trust me, Harold, and take one day at a time. Dwell in my power

and love and be free. Be yourself. Don't allow other people
to run you.

"I will guide you if you will let me. Be aware of my presence in everything. I give you patience, love, joy, and peace.
Look to me for answers. I am your Shepherd and will lead
you. Follow me only. Do not ever forget this. Listen and I
will tell you my will. I love you, Harold. I love you! Let it
flow from you, spilling over to all you touch.

"Be not concerned with yourself; you are my responsibility.
I will change you without your hardly knowing it. You are to
love yourself and to love others simply because I love you.
Take your eyes off yourself; look only to and at me. I lead, I
change, I make, but not when you're trying; I won't fight
your efforts.

"You are mine, Harold. Let me have the joy of making
you like Christ. Let me give you joy, peace, and kindness.
No one else can. You're not your own. You have been
bought with blood and now belong to me. Your only demand
is to look to me and only me, never to yourself and never to
others. Don't struggle. Relax in my love. Stop trying. Let me
make you what I want. My will is perfect, my love sufficient.
Look to me. I love you, Harold."

Again and again I read those words to find encouragement
in weary hours. They helped me view my illness as a challenge rather than an irritation or attack. They also taught
me to deal with everything from God's perspective. Because
of that I have learned many precious truths, such as the
importance of prayer. The most difficult prayer I offered was
the one expressing my willingness to have everything God's
way instead of my own.

Suffering also taught me a special kind of godly patience.
David wrote, "Wait on the Lord; Be of good courage, and
He shall strengthen your heart; Wait, I say, on the Lord!"
(Psalm 27:14). As I sought the Lord, He turned waiting into
a profitable experience.

Through affliction God also drew me closer to Himself. I
learned to trust him more completely, and that is the most

difficult aspect of the Christian life. I found that God is a comfort. He is personally involved in our lives, especially when we are suffering. He permits weaknesses and trials, so we may come to depend totally upon His strength as we cast our cares upon Him. Trials provide an opportunity to know God better, and knowing God is the secret to a full and blessed life.

A TROPHY OF
GOD'S GRACE

One sultry day in the summer of 1985, I was returning home to Atlanta after vacationing in Florida. As I came through Savannah, Georgia, something kept pulling me to go by my old prison seventy-five miles away.

Rain fell in torrents as I drove around the Georgia State Penitentiary. A massive renovation program had brought many changes to the prison, but I located the building where I first trusted Christ. I parked near the building that housed death row and looked up at the window in the cell where I spent six lonely months.

I walked toward the prison graveyard. The rain slammed down with a fierceness I had rarely seen as I walked among the small numbered crosses. If an inmate's body is not claimed within twenty-four hours after death, he is buried in the prison graveyard in a wooden coffin built in the prison carpentry shop. Inmates on work detail dig the grave and the prison chaplain offers the final words. A cross marks the grave.

Searching for something indefinable, I came to a special marker. Suddenly a memory surfaced, and I was surprised both by its poignancy and by the fact that I had forgotten it. Suddenly I was back in prison. The year was 1972, and I was helping with the burial of an inmate friend.

My heart was heavy as I thought aloud, "He doesn't even have a tombstone; he's just a number."

"That's all you are, a number! A bunch of animals!" snapped the guard. "You're not even a citizen of the United States. Society doesn't care. Your own family doesn't care. Nobody cares!"

Boiling rage inside drove me to action. The men who died here would have a memorial. Several of us made arrangements through the chaplain's office to purchase a marker, and other inmates helped me collect money. The inscription was carefully worded:

> Georgia State Penitentiary Cemetery. The first burial was on December 20, 1937. The state provides a Christian burial for all deceased inmates for whom private or family burial arrangements are not available. The Savior said, 'Come unto me, and I will give you rest.' These men lie here in peaceful anonymity. Ezekiel 18:22: 'None of the transgressions which he has committed shall be remembered against him. Because of the righteousness which he has done, he shall live.' This memorial marker was provided by inmates July 1, 1972.

Grief flooded my spirit as I considered the opportunity given to every sinner in Ezekiel 18:23: "Do I have any pleasure at all that the wicked should die?" says the Lord God, "and not that he should turn from his ways and live?" Surely the wicked man would be saved if he turned from his wicked ways. But the men lying here did *not* turn! Most of them suffered violent deaths. Did they have a Christian burial and lie in peaceful anonymity? It was a comforting thought, but it was a farce.

As sheets of rain poured from above, I fell to my knees and wept for the poor souls in the prison graveyard who never knew the saving name of Jesus.

Thank you, God, for freedom. For life. For salvation. For healing! Have mercy on the men who are locked within these prison walls. Forgive me for not having compassion. Forgive society for not caring.

Oh, God, where are the churches? Shouldn't Christians be involved? Shouldn't your people care about these unwanted men?

It occurred to me that the church is the biggest tombstone of all—a monument among the dead. When Jesus died on the cross to save us from sin, His purpose was not only to provide a way for us to enter heaven but also to make us more like Himself, that we might minister to others in His name. He instructed us to feed the hungry, to clothe the naked, to visit those who are sick and in prison. Christ wants us to be instruments through whom the needs of people can be met. We can never have the kind of life He wants us to have until we learn to love others in His name.

We seem to forget verses such as 1 John 3:17–18: "But whoever has this world's goods, and sees his brother in need, and shuts up his heart from him, how does the love of God abide in him? My little children, let us not love in word or in tongue, but in deed and in truth."

How can we say we love Jesus if we do not care about the suffering people whom Jesus loves? We have excess wealth, yet refuse to share it with those who are starving. Being Christlike is caring about the hungry, the naked, the sick, and the imprisoned.

To be sure, God used my prison experience to save my life. At the time of my arrest, I was hell-bent on self-destruction, and there is no doubt that, had I continued in that direction, I would have become a drug addict and an alcoholic. Ultimately, mine would have been a life of crime. I'm convinced that if I had not been arrested, I would have fallen to such a low point physically and mentally that I could not have overcome. I might have even killed somebody.

If the verdict had been different—not guilty—I still would never have touched another drop of liquor, having learned my lesson going through the trial. But it took those years in prison—living with the most powerless people in society—to realize there was more to life than what I had.

Prison. It is forever a part of me, for in that decade, I

lived a lifetime. I've relived that experience a million times.
The anger. The hatred. The terror. The utter hopelessness.

Because God is my Redeemer, He has redeemed those
awful times, replacing rage and hatred with love for those
who hurt. Replacing terror with confidence in His sover-
eignty. Replacing hopelessness with hope.

I could never repay Jesus Christ for what He has done for
me. To lose everything, to be reduced in life to nothing, to
be among the most powerless people on earth, then suddenly
to be given everything! He became the Living Answer to all
of my doubts, all of my pains, all of my problems. But He
did not do it alone.

In Romans 10, Paul asks some powerful questions about
those who need to know the Good News of Jesus. He says,

> Everyone who calls on the name of the Lord will be saved.
> How, then, can they call on the one they have not believed
> in? And how can they believe in the one of whom they have
> not heard? And how can they hear without someone preach-
> ing to them? (Rom. 10:13–14, NIV).

It is because people like Cliff Miller, Clebe McClary,
Bobby Richardson, and Bob Norris chose to live out the
Incarnation in my life that I have been set free, not only
from the physical prison, but from the shackles of sin and
despair.

Thank God they shared love when I had no one else,
stood with me when I needed a friend, taught me about faith
by taking a public stand for Christ. They lived for Jesus, and
their lives challenged mine.

Where is the church? Where are the Cliff Millers, the
Russell Moores, the Clebe McClarys?

People are waiting to see what we will do with our lives.
If God could use a shepherd boy to witness to a king, and
ex-convict 62345 to witness to prisoners, parents, and teens,
surely He can use you. There is no limit to what He can do
with an individual who is faithful and follows Him, wherever
He may lead.